THE ENDLESS PATH
A Memoir

Laurie Plessala Duperier
and
Ganimedes Duperier

We hope that you enjoy the Path !

Laurie &

"Anything can happen if you let it."
Mary Poppins

April 19, 2012

Beloved Ganimedes,

I remember the day that we met—August 31, 1997. You looked right at me, your handsome face a mixture of curiosity and anticipation, neither of us quite certain what was going to happen next. Who was going to make the next move? Take the next step? Even at such a young age, you had a penetrating gaze, always sizing up everyone you met in one glance, as if to say, "Don't bother trying to hide who you really are. I see you quite clearly." I never could have imagined on that day in 1997 who and what we would become years later. What at first seemed like a chance meeting grew to feel like a destiny from which I did not want to escape, and could not have escaped had I tried.

I loved you the moment I first saw you, but if I am honest about it, I didn't always like you very much in the early days. When we were younger, it felt like you were always testing me, trying to figure out which of your challenges I would take on and which ones I would back down from. In Spain, they test the young bulls to draw out their character in order to determine who is fit for the bullring—who will back down from a poke with a stick and who will charge the person poking him. I often felt you were putting me through a similar trial. I'm not sure which reaction you wanted from me, but I think you eventually concluded that if it was important to me, I would take on the battle. Must have been like looking in the mirror for you, because you were just the same. You did not become a warrior. You were born one.

1

I suppose we practiced on each other more than necessary, but all of those practice battles came in handy when the real wars started, don't you think? You knew all along that while not everything is worth fighting for, some things are worth fighting for with all that you have and all that you are. You taught me that. I will never understand why there was so much illness, why we had to fight for your life over and over again, and in turn fight for our hearts to be together, but we did. And we fought well.

Of course, in the "in between" time, when we were just living our lives without illness or worry, you always made me laugh and did your best to keep me present in the moment. How could my mind venture anywhere else when you kissed me all over my face until I had to just surrender in hysterics because it tickled so much and you just wouldn't stop? What could be more fun than watching you sing to your favorite flamenco song, or seeing you run with abandon just for the fun of it? All those happy strolls in the vineyards of Switzerland, taking in the natural beauty of the land—those were great times.

In the end, there were too many battles, too many wars. I'd like to think that we could have done just fine without half of them. Would we have been the same without all the near-death moments? Would we have understood each other as well, "breathed together as one," as you say? I don't know. It is unknowable. The path was laid out before us and we walked it, hearts in each other's hands, until we loved each other so much that I was never sure where I ended and where you began.

Although there are many things that I do not know, there are some things that I know with every fiber of my being. Meeting you was the best thing that ever happened to me. Sharing almost fifteen years with you was the great privilege of my life. It was an honor to hold you when you were unsteady, support you when you were weak, and comfort you when you were sick. It was an honor to fight with you, side by side. It was also an honor to just take a walk with you and accompany you on a day when nothing special happened, because just being with you was special. You carried yourself with more grace and dignity than anyone I have ever known. Indeed, you died with more dignity than many people ever manifest in their lifetimes.

So what can I say to you now? You have gone. I am left here without you and I have moments when I think I might go crazy from missing you and not being able to stroke your face or hold your paw in my hand again. I have no words for the anguish that washes over me some days. I think that I won't be able to bear it. It is too hard. I am not up to the task.

And then I remember to breathe. I feel myself breathe with you, even though you are so far away, and my heart fills with gratitude. So in the end all I can say is, "Thank you." Thank you for loving me just as I am, for helping me to realize who I really am, and for patiently staying by my side while I tried to find my way through this life with you, Juan Carlos, and Bacchus. Thank you for teaching me how to fight with all my being when the cause is right. Thank you for breaking open my heart so that I could know what it is like to love someone so completely and without hesitation, knowing that my heart was always safe with you.

I hope that I can be even half the person you turned out to be. And more than anything, I hope that we find each other again across the "mist of time" you always talked about.

I believe that we will. And while I am still here, I will do my best to honor your life by making the most of what you taught me and by sharing it with others.

I will love you until the end of time.

Laurie

Chapter 1

I hope this [book] will inspire people. I like to think that this could be a start of the human race understanding the animal kingdom. I hope people will read this to their dogs and cats and horses so they know they have a voice. They can actually be heard. They can communicate their thoughts and feelings.

We are all of us alive and are all connected to the same consciousness. Life is life, souls are souls.

Ganimedes

Ganimedes, or "Gunny" for short, was a chocolate Labrador retriever who, as you will come to see, had hopes and dreams for his life, and had a lot to say.

Even before he was able to communicate in complete sentences, Gunny was talking *all the time*. I didn't hear him in terms of an audible voice, other than his barking to demand service. But if you have ever lived with a dog, you know that he or she is communicating with you constantly. The only question is whether or not you understand.

There was no mistaking when Gunny was happy, when he wanted dinner, when he wanted to play, when he wanted to be left alone, or—God help us all—when he was displeased. He most often communicated by staring at me and then looking over in the direction he wanted me to go: look up the stairs, ready to go to bed; look in the kitchen, time for a snack. If "the look" didn't work, he would gently take my hand in his mouth and lead me to where he wanted to go. If he was feeling impatient, sometimes he would just go get his leash and give it to me as a way of telling me to take him outside. And on occasion, he literally nipped at my butt, driving me like a cow into the room that contained what he wanted. He once herded me into the kitchen all the way from the upstairs bedroom because I was five minutes late with his breakfast.

Occasionally, he would just stare into my eyes for long periods of time, wagging his tail, clearly talking to me, and I would have to shrug my shoulders and say, "Sorry, buddy, I just don't understand what you're saying." This was often met with what I can only describe as a, "Hrmph," and then he would walk off in frustration at my lack of ability to understand him—making clear that the failing was mine, not his.

At the risk of stating the obvious, I am not an animal communicator. There are many people who are. I don't know how they each work, but they all seem to have an ability to forge a telepathic connection, a shared knowing, with animals. Telepathic communication has no geographic boundaries and no language—no words. It is a pure thought connection that can be "heard" across a room or across the country.

As I have now learned, every animal, just like every person, is unique and has his or her own *voice*. My voice is different from yours, of course. The mere fact that we are the same species doesn't mean that we think the same, feel the same, or talk the same. Why would it be different for non-human animals?

The fact that I can even raise the question represents quite an evolution on my part. I spent two decades as a corporate lawyer, dealing in a very structured world of irrefutable facts. But on some level, I have always believed that animals can communicate. After all, the first book that I fell in love with when I was nine years old was *Charlotte's Web*. However, until Gunny, I don't think that I really ever considered that animals could have articulate and profound observations to share if the right person was listening. Or, shall we say, was able to *hear*. In Gunny's case, Alexandra, my long-time friend who also happens to be clairvoyant, was that right person.

Gunny and Alexandra had met briefly when he was a puppy, but we then moved overseas and they didn't see each other again until he was eleven years old, when she came to visit me outside Washington, D.C., where I live now. During many of Alexandra's visits to Washington, she would spend a day doing psychic readings for various friends of mine who wanted one. She did not work with animals at that time, but only because no one had ever asked!

Since Gunny had had more than his fair share of illness, on one of her visits I asked her to draw Gunny's aura and do an energetic healing to try to help him, just like she did for people. As it turned out, she was able to see Gunny's energy quite easily, and the thing I remember most about that drawing was all the bright green-colored energy under his feet — that boy loved grass more than anything. He liked to lie in it, run in it, roll in it, smell it, and look for disgusting things hidden in it, as often as possible.

As she finished drawing his aura, she heard him speak to her. As Gunny himself would explain it later,

I had watched Alexandra sitting at our dining room table drawing peoples' auras and speaking to them. I'm not sure why I started to pay attention to what she was doing, but now that I think about it, I liked the way the room felt and looked. I decided I would try to speak with her about me ... I like that she can hear me. It's so easy. She's interesting.

To be clear, Gunny didn't "speak" English. Alexandra understood the thoughts that he conveyed to her and she expressed her understanding of those thoughts in English, because that is the language that *she* speaks. While she expressed the thoughts he shared with her in English, the things she said sounded nothing like the way Alexandra talks:

I want a new bed. Mine is not comfortable. I want a red ball to play with. I want Laurie to explain to me what stars are. I sit outside at night and see them but I don't know what they are. I want her to talk to me the way she talks to her friends. Why doesn't she talk to me like that?

8

If Gunny was going to speak, it didn't surprise me in the least that his first words were a to-do list for me.

Predictably, I immediately began fulfilling his wish list. I went to Orvis to get him a giant orthopedic bed so that he would be more comfortable. We went to PetSmart together so he could walk up and down the toy aisle and pick out the red ball that I *knew* he was never going to play with, and never did. (He didn't like to fetch. He found it pointless.) I lay down with him one night in the grass, under a clear sky, and did my best to explain to him what stars were. I began talking to him in complete sentences, telling him about my day, telling him everything I thought and felt.

What started as a "lark" (his word, not mine) one day in my dining room grew into something none of us could have anticipated. For the next several years, Gunny and Alexandra spoke occasionally, usually at my request, and usually about how he was feeling or if he was willing to undergo one medical treatment or another. He was always forthcoming with his opinions, but the conversations never seemed to trend to the philosophical — they were more transactional: "*Yes, I want the surgery if it is necessary for me to live,*" or "*My back hurts,*" and so on. Back then, he sounded simple and dog-like.

That all changed when he became gravely ill at thirteen years old. It is a story that we will get to, but something changed in him during the course of that illness and his recovery. Perhaps being so close to death gave him a heightened awareness; an awakening of sorts. I truly do not know what happened. But from that point forward, the clarity of his thinking, his choice of words, his ability to remember things,

9

and the nature of his comments when he spoke to Alexandra evolved rapidly. His words were astonishing, and much more complex than in their earlier conversations.

In light of that, I asked Alexandra to do something she had never done before: "Please interview Gunny on a list of subjects that I have come up with to get his thoughts and feelings about them." She didn't laugh, but she was a bit wary because this was a mighty strange assignment. She said she would do it on one condition—"I am going to write down whatever he says, as he says it, and will not change anything or edit anything even if what he says is not what you want to hear." I agreed.

The list of subjects I had put together ranged from, "What was the best moment of your life?" to "What is life's purpose as you see it?" I yearned to understand more about his perspective on his life; *our* life. We had a relationship of equals by that point. I no longer really noticed that he was in a dog suit and I was in a person suit. We were a single unit. Two who fit together as one. It was unconventional at best, and I needed him to help me make sense of it all.

But the driving factor in asking her to interview him was that I felt that we should write a book—*this* book—about our life together. For years, people who knew us and who knew of our adventures had said to me, "You really should write a book." I laughed it off because what on earth made my life so special that anyone would want to read about it? Over time, however, I realized that while I was not so special, *he* was. *We* were.

So having agreed to participate in this crazy project, Alexandra told Gunny that I wanted him to share his thoughts about a variety of subjects because I wanted to write a book with him about our life together. His response? *"Oh goody. I get to write my memoirs."* Pardon me, Gunny, but it is *our* memoirs. (He always was a bit of a narcissist.)

Once Gunny started this writing project, words poured out of him for hours at a time. He had had many years to observe and to think. He was now ready to talk about his life and our journey together. I had always had a lot of respect for Gunny, but I had never imagined that stuffed inside a chocolate Labrador retriever body was a being not so different from me, and who had rather humbling insight into life.

Gunny and Alexandra spoke regularly over a six-month period of time, whenever Gunny was in the mood. Alexandra would contact him, let him know which question she would like to discuss next, and Gunny would often reflect on it and then contact her when he was ready to talk—even if that meant he woke her up in the middle of the night in Los Angeles. Although they continued their conversations until the day that he died, he dictated the bulk of what you are reading here during the last year of his life. They discussed one by one each subject I had identified, although he often went off on tangents and offered up his point of view on questions that I had not thought to ask. He made sure he talked about what was important to him, and humored me by answering the questions that he found naïve or simple. The process of talking to Alexandra stimulated thoughts and feelings, and in some instances, memories of times long ago—much the

11

way asking your grandfather about one event in his life might lead him to reflect on other events, resulting in his sharing a treasure trove of memories and feelings that you otherwise might never have known.

I have done my best to explain the process by which Gunny spoke to Alexandra in the hopes that it will enhance your understanding of our journey and how this all came to pass. But I want to be clear that Gunny and I didn't write this book to convince you of anything. We have no agenda. We just want to tell you our story and have you walk with us for a while on our beautiful, and endless, path.

Let's begin at the beginning.

Chapter 2

When I was a puppy, I was caught up in the body, the awkward moments of growing, coordination, feeling my way with Juan Carlos and Laurie, doing what I was told, not doing what I was told, not sure of what was happening. I always felt I was floundering about, not always making Laurie and Juan Carlos pleased by my actions. I didn't like having to do what they wanted. I was pissed at being me. At that time I would have said my life had no real purpose at all. Like any child, eating, sleeping, and being was all there was.

Ganimedes

Ganimedes was born on July 5, 1997. He was my wedding gift from my husband, Juan Carlos. The fact that I have a husband is a bit surprising to me, actually. I spent so many years studying and working long hours in big law firms that I did not have time for much else in my life. I was married to my job in many ways, and I was pretty content with my life despite it all. Until I went to Spain in 1995.

I was living in Los Angeles at that point, and one day while reading the *Los Angeles Times* I saw an ad offering a two-for-one airfare deal to fly from Los Angeles to Madrid. I had a close friend from law school who was living in Madrid at the time, so my cousin and I decided to go together. Cheap airfare, free place to stay, and a local to show us around. I called my friend to say, "Guess what? I'm coming to Madrid in February!" She said, "Guess what? We're moving back to the United States in December." Uh oh.

We went to Madrid anyway, and without my friend there to guide us, we roamed around looking for interesting things to do, with a lot of emphasis on eating and drinking. One evening we stumbled onto a little restaurant and bar near the Plaza Mayor called the *Mesón de la Guitarra*. There, sitting at the bar, laughing and clapping to flamenco music, was Juan Carlos. I certainly didn't know in that moment that he would become my husband, but he was nice, spoke decent English, and chatted with us during the evening when he wasn't playing guitar and clapping *palmas* with his friends to the flamenco guitar.

Among the things Juan Carlos spoke to us about that night was the Camino de Santiago, known in English as the Way of Saint James. It is an ancient Christian pilgrimage across the north of Spain that dates back to the Middle Ages. People have been walking the Path for over a thousand years, bringing their aspirations, joys, and troubles with them in hopes of sorting it all out. Walking in beautiful countryside all day, day after day, is a great way to figure out almost anything. For Juan Carlos, it is an opportunity to reflect on his life and think about how he can improve himself. He had just returned from walking part of the Path a few months before we met and said he was looking forward to going again. I naïvely said,

"That sounds so interesting. I would love to do that one day." Had I understood how difficult it can be to walk the Camino, I would have said, "I would love to do that with a pack mule and a personal masseuse."

Juan Carlos and I saw each other several times before I left Spain and vowed to stay in touch. To sum up for the women reading this: I met a professional soccer player in a bar in Spain while on vacation, where he spoke to me about walking five hundred miles to become a better person, and I married him. To the men reading this, I say, "You see, you just never know what will interest a girl."

I moved back to Washington, D.C. shortly after we met, and Juan Carlos and I dated across continents for over a year. We were not longing to be married; we were happy like we were. I was not a woman who had dreamed of her wedding for years, nor did I feel a social pressure to marry. We would have been fine living together. But as a lawyer, I found the Immigration and Naturalization Service's views on our being together persuasive. We had to get married in order for Juan Carlos to be able to legally stay in the United States for longer than three months at a time. So we pulled together all the letters, photos, and other evidence of the legitimacy of our relationship, went for an interview with the INS, and got a fiancé visa which allowed him to enter the United States for the purpose of getting married.

We married on May 3, 1997. Juan Carlos and I had agreed that after the wedding we would start looking for a puppy and that the puppy would be my wedding present from him. (As it turns out, May 3rd was quite likely the day

15

that Gunny's mom ended up pregnant.) Juan Carlos and I thought that a Labrador retriever would be a good breed of dog for us. Juan Carlos likes to run and is outdoors a lot, so the dog would get plenty of exercise and lots of retrieving time. And Labs are usually great with people, kids, and other dogs. We looked in the local paper and saw some ads for chocolate Labs for sale by a breeder. Juan Carlos made an appointment and went to pick out my wedding present; I stayed home and prayed that he would choose wisely.

There were two male chocolate Lab puppies for sale on the day that Juan Carlos visited the breeder. He held the first puppy, who just sat in his lap and did not do much. The breeder then handed him the puppy with a green ribbon around his neck, and that dog crawled up his chest and bit his ear. The choice was clear—he bought the one with the green ribbon and agreed to come back in about two weeks' time, when the puppy was fully weaned, to pick him up.

We had already decided on a name and a nickname. The dog's name would be Ganimedes (Ganymede in English), in honor of Juan Carlos' father. Juan Carlos' dad had always called him "Ganimedes" because Juan Carlos was the one at the dinner table who filled his father's wine glass, and in Greek mythology, Ganimedes was the wine bearer to the gods. A brief primer from Wikipedia:

> In Greek mythology, Ganymede (Greek: Γανυμήδης, *Ganymēdēs*) is a divine hero who [was] abducted by Zeus, in the form of an eagle, to serve as cupbearer in Olympus. Zeus granted

him eternal youth and immortality and the office of cupbearer to the gods. Some interpretations of the myth treat it as an allegory of the human soul aspiring to immortality.

Had Wikipedia existed in 1997 and had I read that, perhaps I would have had a better idea of who was coming to live with me. Instead, I was very focused on finding a nickname that was easy to pronounce when we were at the dog park. We settled on Gunny.

We brought Ganimedes home in August. It was a rocky start, as Gunny evidently was unfamiliar with the character traits of a Labrador retriever—likes to retrieve, easy to train, and eager to please. Really? The books didn't say anything about destroying any and everything in sight and staring at me defiantly when requested to sit. Eager to please? In the first six months, he ate several pairs of shoes, his leather leash, the arm of a chair, the legs of a coffee table, and all of the stuffing out of one of the sofa cushions. The latter he continued to do *after* I walked into the room, pausing only momentarily to look at me as if to say, *"Did you want something?"* before returning to his work on my cushion. He also made clear that our "commands" of sit, come, down, and stay would be entertained as mere suggestions, to be agreed to or not only after much reflection on his part. Under no circumstance, ever, would he retrieve a ball. He did, however, enjoy watching me throw it in the backyard, retrieve it myself, then throw it again—which I did daily—hoping that he would get the hang of it. He usually observed my self-retrieving sessions while lying down under a shady tree, often while chewing on a blade of grass and laughing quietly under his breath.

These things all happened after we hired not one, but two, dog trainers. The second one, who had been a dog trainer in the Marines, matter-of-factly pronounced him the most stubborn dog that he had ever met. It wasn't just a puppy trait. It was who he was; and he never changed.

Who would have guessed that all the skills of persuasion I had honed over years of practicing law would prove most useful at home when trying to reason with my dog? *"Doing what I was told. Not doing what I was told,"* he said. When, dear boy, did you *ever* do what you were told? We either persuaded Gunny to do something, or we bribed him with food. He did not do something because we told him to do it. In fact, our telling him to do something seemed to actually be a source of amusement for him. In turn, he was a source of amusement for us, even when he was exasperating.

Had the three of us realized then that he was basically a person who got stuffed into a dog suit this time around, it all would have made more sense. But at the time, we were clueless.

Chapter 3

I didn't come into this life with the awareness of hopes and dreams. None of us do. Looking at the past, I guess I hoped to get tasty things to eat, approval and affection from my family. There have been many times I just wanted to feel good and be outside and run around, lay under a shady tree, play, eat, affection, all the basics.

Being with Laurie is a given. I liked going places with Juan Carlos. It made me feel important. He has been a good friend and very kind and makes me laugh. I like when he sings because that is how I know he is happy, just like when I play with a shoe. I have grown to understand and love him deeply. When I was younger he showed me how to have fun. He is so different from Laurie and me. We mostly live in our heads, he in his body — although he sometimes surprises me, catches me off guard with something he says or does that is quite perceptive or philosophical. I like how carefree he can be and the long walks and the games he likes to play. He can be happy doing nothing at all, and it's been a good lesson for me, since in living this dog life there is a lot of time for that. Now I just dream about my past and think about what my future might be.

Ganimedes

Our first two years with Gunny were full of change. During that period, I made my first pilgrimage on the Camino de Santiago, I left my job at a law firm, we bought our first house, and Juan Carlos started his own soccer school and summer soccer camp for kids—more or less in that order. Gunny was my training buddy for the Camino. For two months we walked two or three hours a day, several days a week, in order to prepare. I would pack lunch for us and off we'd go to explore the local nature trails. It was quiet time to just be together, which we cherished.

I walked a small part of the Camino that first time to clear my head and prepare for my new job. Although the Camino was more physically difficult than I had expected, walking all day for five days in beautiful countryside, connecting with interesting people along the Camino, and just having quiet time to think, was glorious. I was hooked, and I knew that I wanted to go back some day.

When we returned from the Camino, we settled into our new house where Gunny met Sam, a young Lab about his age. They became fast friends. Up until then, Gunny had not been very lucky at making dog friends; other dogs were always kind of mean to him, for no apparent reason. He was the kid on the playground who got bullied. So Sam, who actually looked up to him, was really special. When Gunny smelled Sam come out of his house two doors down, he would start dancing around at the door and whining, so excited that his friend was on his way to play. They would chase each other from yard to yard for over an hour every morning and evening, so long as the humans continued to watch them — and in the evening the humans doing the watching were Sam's dad and Juan Carlos, accompanied by a bottle of cognac. Half the fun for them was having their people see them play.

The only thing Gunny loved as much as playing with Sam was singing flamenco. His love for flamenco was rather inexplicable, unless you believe that he inherited it from Juan Carlos. We discovered his passion when one day, out of nowhere, Gunny started howling like a wolf while standing in the living room. He had never done this before. He stood there, lips puckered, head held high, wailing away. We looked around the house, but couldn't figure out what on earth was making him howl like that. It stopped after a few minutes, and we didn't think much more about it until a couple of nights later when he did the same thing again.

It took us weeks to figure out what was inspiring Gunny to sing. Turns out, it was a particular song by Remedios Amaya, a famous Spanish flamenco singer, that caused him to howl. Only that song. Only the chorus. Once we figured it out, all we had to say was, "Gunny, do you want to sing?" and he knew that we were going to play his favorite song. He would howl away to the music, and then we'd give him cookies as his reward. His singing became everyone's favorite party trick, and he gave a solid performance every time. He sang as long as he had a voice, and when he lost his voice in his later years, he would still stand there, pucker his lips, and howl to that song—although only a faint whisper came out. Something in the music just moved his soul.

Over time, Gun stopped eating shoes and started playing with them instead. We always knew when Gunny was happy because he would get a shoe in his mouth and dance around the room. Part of the reason he liked to do this was because stealing a shoe caused us to chase him around the house to get it back, and he thought that was the best game ever. We would "run" behind him when he took off with the shoe, saying, "I'm going to get you," in a sing-song voice, while he did circles dancing around the coffee table. I remember perfectly the last time in his life that he stole a shoe and danced—when a few months before he died, I told him that Bacchus, his brother, was coming home from the hospital.

A lot of the tension with Gunny worked itself out in those first two years. The main reason for this was because Juan Carlos and I became more obedient. He was adorable, he didn't usually ask for wildly unreasonable things, and it gave us tremendous pleasure to make him happy. It also gave *him* tremendous pleasure for us to make him happy, so it was a win-win.

About a year after we bought our new house and we were finally settled in, I was offered a job by a client of my old law firm. One of my former colleagues worked there, and he called to ask if I wanted to move to Hong Kong to work for them. A job like that was definitely on the ladder to success and sounded like a great opportunity. After all, a person only gets offered the chance to move to Hong Kong once in a lifetime, if *ever*, and I really wanted to do it. I expressed only one concern. "Do I have to quarantine my dog? Because if I do, we can't go."

Chapter 4

I see China differently now when I think back. It had unusual and different colors, smells, and feelings. When we were there, Laurie was gone a lot and there was always a quiet, unknowing uncertainty. The sea seemed endless and the rocky beach by the house was uncomfortable to walk on. There was too much light, too much water, too much space. I also worried there was nothing on the other side of the sea but more water and nothingness. When both Laurie and Juan Carlos were gone I would feel I was in a sort of limbo, isolated, not a lot happened. I wanted to know where boats disappeared to and if Laurie and Juan Carlos were ever going to come back and take us home.

The [housekeeper] who lived with us did feed me some interesting things. As you know, good food always puts me in a better mood. I guess I've always been spoiled one way or another. I see now that hasn't helped my understanding of humility. Looking back I could have used the time more to my advantage but I didn't. I didn't understand why we were even there.

I don't think Juan Carlos liked it that much either,

especially when Laurie was gone. He might [have] thought it was interesting sometimes, but not for long periods of time. He's always happier in Spain.

Ganimedes

Hearing Gunny's views on Hong Kong, many years later, made me sad, because I was truly unaware of how lonely Gunny was during that time.

We moved to Hong Kong when Gunny was two years old, and installed ourselves in a beautiful four-story townhouse with twenty-five-foot-tall windows overlooking the South China Sea. For Gunny, this was *"too much light, too much water, too much space."* For me, it was a gorgeous place to live. I even got the landlord to plant grass where the patio had been so that Gunny would have a place to roll. There is not a lot of grass in Hong Kong, and he had the biggest patch of grass on the island, all to himself.

While Gunny may not have loved his new home, he was very serious about protecting it from what he must have imagined to be invading pirates; every morning at 9:30 a.m., the same fishing boat puttered into our cove and came within twenty yards of our dining room, causing him to bark his fool head off to get the boat to retreat. Much like the mailman was "scared away" every day, the fishing boat went away after a few minutes of hearing him bark, nets full of fish. Some evenings, when things were a little too quiet, we would say, "Gunny, where's the boat?" just to get him riled up and watch him run to the window, barking furiously, searching for the invaders. For a decade after we left Hong Kong, if you said to Gunny, "Where's the boat?" he would run to the nearest window of whatever house we lived in, barking. We found it almost as funny as the flamenco singing, and never tired of playing that trick on him because he fell for it every time.

I traveled all over Asia for my job (resting easy knowing that Gunny was keeping all the pirates at bay in my absence) and was on the road at least half of the time. Juan Carlos often traveled with me, as this was our chance to really explore Asia. Traveling was one of our passions so there was not much to complain about, even though I was working awfully hard. Obviously, Gunny felt differently. Despite the fact that I regularly called home to talk to him (and he always returned the greeting by licking the phone receiver when I said, "Kiss kiss"), he was at home with a housekeeper he hardly knew, feeling left behind.

Gunny wasn't as playful as he had been in the United States, but I just thought it was because he was growing up—and because the horrific heat in Hong Kong most of the year prevented him from playing outside much. As a result, we started to think about getting another dog to keep him company in the air-conditioned house.

Gunny was marvelous, fabulous Gunny, but more aloof and less affectionate than most Labs. I thought a face-licking, rub-my-tummy, throw-the-ball retriever in addition to Gunny might be a nice dog to have around. About that time, my mom called one day just to talk. Amid the chatter she made a comment about how it was finally quieter around her house now that the neighbor's puppies, who had been living outside in a kennel, had all been adopted—except for one. It stopped me cold.

I said, "What do you mean there is only one left?"

She said, "All the puppies were sold except one, and I think they're just going to keep it."

"Is there something wrong with it?"

"Not that I know of," she said.

"Is it a boy or a girl?"

"I don't know," she said. "*Why?*"

Excellent question! And for reasons that would not become obvious until several years later, I said, "I don't know, I just think the dog was not sold because it's supposed to be mine. He's my destiny."

Let's be clear about something here. I was having this conversation with my mother, who lives in Port Arthur, Texas, while I was living in Hong Kong, China. If I were going to get a dog, it did not make a whole lot of sense to get one in Port Arthur from a backyard breeder. But I really and truly felt that this dog that I had never met or seen, not even in a photo, was left behind for me.

So, we did the only rational thing. We flew to Port Arthur at Christmas time to pick him up and ship him to Hong Kong. My generous employer was not crazy enough to pay for such a thing, and the price tag to get my "destiny" to Hong Kong was about $2,500. The neighbor had sold him to me for $75.

As with Gunny, this dog had a name before we even met him. Logically, it was Bacchus, the god of wine, in keeping with the wine-mythology theme. I can assure you, however, that there was never a day that Ganimedes, our wine bearer to the gods, served the god of wine living in *our* house. Quite the opposite. Bacchus took orders from Gunny on the day he arrived, and did not stop following orders until the day that Gunny left this life. (Funny — the same thing happened to me.)

Was Gunny happy to have this new companion? It is hard to say. He was excited about being with Bacchus the first couple of days, but soon thereafter I would swear that when he looked at me, he was saying, *"When will this annoying puppy be leaving?"*

They didn't have much in common back then. They just co-existed — never a fight, but never a love fest, either. Gunny described his feelings about Bacchus in those early years as follows:

> *When Bacchus came along I was jealous at first, but as you know I have come to love him and value him as my friend. Bacchus drove me crazy back then. He was confused and sad a lot and very annoying. I guess we both were in our own way. It wasn't fun when Laurie and Juan Carlos were gone and there wasn't much to be excited about. At the same time we leaned on each other emotionally. He depended on me a lot but I didn't have a lot to say. It was a strange time.*

Bacchus, on the other hand, pretty much adored Gunny from the moment they met, and he seemed happy to let Gun take the lead. In connection with writing this book, I asked Alexandra to speak to Bacchus to get his perspective on some things, including Gunny:

I feel I will never be able to be as smart as he is or as wise. I look up to him. Sometimes he is bossy and I don't want to listen to what he has to say. He has taught me many things, but I don't always understand him. I feel bad when I don't. I like that we have had so many good times together.

My face-licking, tummy-rub-seeking, ball-retrieving Bacchus put a little pep in everyone's step in Hong Kong, including Gunny's. But obviously, they both felt a bit overlooked when we lived there—and they probably were—and for that, I am sorry.

Chapter 5

Through time I have always been a survivor. Isn't that what so much of life is about, having to survive and having the will to endure?

Ganimedes

Until we moved to Hong Kong, I don't think Gunny felt life was about being a "survivor". His puppyhood seemed to have been pretty happy, and to hear him describe it, life had been pretty simple up until then: *"Eating, sleeping, and being was all there was."* But shortly after we moved there, I have to admit, survival became the name of the game.

One day, Juan Carlos took the boys out to a trail that led to a reservoir not far from our house, one of their favorite places to walk. This "trail" was actually paved concrete, but there were a few trees and some interesting things to smell (if you're a dog), even if the concrete was a bother. That is as close to nature as you get on Hong Kong Island.

What started as an ordinary walk that day ended in a fiasco. Juan Carlos and the boys had walked up near the reservoir and were on a fairly narrow part of the concrete path that wound around a rocky point. (Hong Kong Island is essentially a big rock protruding from the sea.) As they rounded that corner, a big Labrador inexplicably came running full speed at Juan Carlos, and although he tried to brace himself against the rock wall, the dog knocked him down, and he split his elbow open down to the bone. As he was trying to get himself together, and while the dog's owner apologized profusely, Juan Carlos realized Bacchus was nowhere in sight. And then he heard non-stop crying and followed the sound.

While Juan Carlos was lying on the ground bleeding, Bacchus thought it would be an ideal moment to jump into the reservoir for a swim—not knowing, of course, that there was no way out once he jumped in. He had been swimming there on other occasions, but on this day, the water level was low and the wall of the reservoir was at least three feet above the water line—a sheer face with no foothold. Bacchus couldn't touch bottom to jump out, so he was treading water and clawing at the wall, ripping apart his nails and crying.

Juan Carlos jumped into the reservoir, and standing on his tippy toes, lifted Bacchus far enough up in the air for Bacchus to get a grip on the top of the wall and pull himself out. Having gone from bleeding, to wet and bleeding, Juan Carlos then pulled himself up the wall to get back to dry land. Bacchus' toenails and front paws were a mess, and Juan Carlos' elbow needed stitches. Through it all, Gunny watched quietly, and then walked back to the car with his wounded family.

Juan Carlos called to tell me what had happened, and we agreed that he would take a taxi downtown to the doctor to get stitches for his elbow. I left work to take Bacchus to the vet to mend his paws. At the last moment, I put Gunny in the car with Bacchus, because I thought the vet should take a look at him, too, since he had been a little "off".

For the previous week at least, I had felt that Gunny was not quite himself, but I couldn't have been more specific than that. I was not a super-experienced dog owner, and I did not know then that sometimes the sense that something is not quite right, and whether you act promptly on that instinct, can be the difference in your dog's living or dying.

Once the vet tended to Bacchus, she took a look at Gunny. I told her what I've just told you – "He's just not himself. I can't tell you more than that." In less than five minutes she diagnosed him as anemic due to a tick-borne disease called babesiosis. Ticks were everywhere in the tropical climate of Hong Kong, and Gunny was a tick magnet. I had put tick repellant on him many times, but we still found ticks on him regularly. Apparently, one of those ticks bore the babesia parasite and had infected him. There are various reactions a dog can have to babesia, and in Gunny's case, it caused him to be very anemic (a deficiency of red blood cells). Babesia is not so common in the United States, or at least it wasn't back then, but the vets in Hong Kong saw dogs die from it every week. The key was catching it early, and they felt that we had caught it in time and that Gunny would likely recover. They injected him with a drug called imidocarb to kill the parasite, put him on a course of antibiotics, and told us to give him plenty of rest.

Sure enough, he felt better in a few weeks, and it seemed the drugs had worked and the worst was behind us. What scared me the most was that I didn't know how much longer

I would have waited to take Gunny to the vet had Bacchus not injured himself and needed medical attention. How "not himself" would I have watched Gunny get before I made an appointment?

Bacchus' jumping into that reservoir had saved Gunny's life, without a doubt. Do I think Bacchus did it on purpose, knowing that would get us to the vet? Not in the least. I think he saw water and wanted to swim. Do I think that Bacchus jumped into the water *on that particular day*, before it was too late to save Gunny, because of fate or serendipity? Having had years to think about it and having lived through all the things that later came to pass, I guess I do. What I know for sure is that it was not the last time Bacchus saved Gunny's life.

Chapter 6

When we go to see any of the vets, there are other animals around who are ill or hurt, and when I look at them at the mercy of the doctors and the people holding their leashes, I wonder how we came to this state of being.

Seeing them all makes me want to help them but also makes me wonder if we would be better off living on our own, taking care of ourselves. What kind of life would that be? I haven't come to any conclusions yet, I'm just taking a look at the possibilities. Would I have been happy as a free agent in the wild? Would I have had friends? Would I have had a family of my own? Would total freedom but a much shorter life be enough?

Animals communicate differently than people; that is obvious, I know, but there is more to it than that. We have instincts that connect us together, to the earth beneath our feet and the sky above and the energy of things. Living a domesticated life has a lot of plusses, but we miss out on our true nature.

Ganimedes

I can imagine Gunny living on his own, except for one detail—food. It is inconceivable to me that this gentle boy, who never hurt a fly, would go out into the forest and kill something for dinner. Nor would he find it acceptable to rummage around through garbage on the street, as that would be beneath him. Of course, being Gunny, he probably would figure out a way to live "on his own" but still get someone else to provide regular meals. Oh wait! He did. *Me.*

Gunny was a very independent soul. It was very clear that the thing he liked least about being a dog was the loss of control over his life, and he talked about it repeatedly in his conversations with Alexandra. As a result, he did not miss an opportunity to exercise control over his life—and mine—when he could. If I attempted to pet him and he wasn't in the mood for company, he would give a heavy sigh, get up, and go find a new place to rest on the other side of the room. When he was in the mood for affection, though, he would lick my face, nuzzle me, and make me laugh for eons. We lived daily life in large part on his terms.

Bacchus, on the other hand, rolled over to give us his tummy if we so much as walked through a room he was in. He was a truly adorable boy. There was never a moment when Bacchus didn't want love and affection—he was a "real" Lab. And he was a get-along, happy-go-lucky guy. He would do anything his brother told him to do, usually without complaint, but in any event he did it. As Bacchus told you earlier, Gunny was bossy. Everyone is in agreement about that.

Now, back to the story.

Gun recovered from the babesiosis, and as soon as he had the okay from the Hong Kong vets, he and Bacchus climbed into their jumbo travel crates and caught a Swissair flight from Hong Kong to our new home—Lausanne, Switzerland. I had been transferred to the international headquarters of the company there, so we were off on our next adventure in December of 2002. This transfer was another step on my career ladder, and we were excited to live in such a beautiful place and take a break from the crowds and pollution in Hong Kong.

We had some good moments in Switzerland, no doubt. Living right above Lake Geneva with a view of the Alps to greet us every morning was no small thing. The country was beautiful; the air was clear; the flowers were amazing. We lived in the vineyards on the hillside and walked in the midst of them most every day.

For Juan Carlos and the boys, the main benefit of living in Switzerland was its proximity to Spain. We had a little townhouse on the Costa del Sol, and they went there often. Spain meant time to enjoy the sun, the beach, and the temperate weather, and it gave Juan Carlos a chance to see his friends and family. It was two days' drive from Switzerland to the Costa del Sol, and they spent the night in the same place each time because it was one of the few hotels that allowed dogs back in 2003. They always had the same set-up at the hotel—one room, three single beds. And the boys always chose their beds first. The one time I made the road trip with them, it created havoc because there was only one bed left for the boys. I don't remember for sure, but it would not surprise me if Gunny made Bacchus sleep on the floor because he wasn't going to share his bed.

For the boys, those trips were great adventure. As Gunny recalls it, *"I remember driving with my head out the window, the wind on my face. I remember being with Juan Carlos and his brother and his wife. They have been good to Bacchus and me."* When we *all* went to Spain, it was our happiest time together. *"There have been some great dog moments in Spain. [Laurie] seemed happier there, at times more than anywhere we have been,"* Gunny said.

I agree. One of the reasons it was always a happy time was because usually when I was in Spain, I wasn't working! We went down to the beach every day. Bacchus retrieved his toy from the sea over and over again, and Gunny hunted in the sand for disgusting things to roll in or eat. You could see the pure joy on Gunny's face when the wind blew his ears up—he looked like the wind might carry him away like the Flying Nun, smiling as he took flight. To him, the ocean "stank of freedom," and as you now know, freedom was one of the things he treasured most.

When I was not able to go with them to Spain, I was left alone in the cold in Lausanne, where the supermarkets closed at 6 p.m. and I worked until 8 p.m. And while the countryside was beautiful, the people could be difficult. There were lots of rules, written and unwritten, and I never found the Swiss to be very welcoming of foreigners. So my time in Switzerland tended to be very lonely.

On top of it all, Juan Carlos had to leave every summer to run his summer soccer camp in Washington, D.C., which left me to take care of the boys alone while trying to keep up with my ridiculous work schedule. Every now and then, the boys came with me to work. (While the Swiss didn't care much for foreigners, they were very welcoming of dogs.) And other days, I dashed home as early as I could to feed and walk them, and then worked from my home office in the evening. I found it overwhelming to manage it all when Juan Carlos was away.

One particular summer evening, I discovered just how close I was to the edge, and how little Gunny was doing to help. When we came in from our evening walk, I took a baked whole chicken out of the fridge, intending to have dinner. Something distracted me, and when I later returned to the kitchen and lifted up the foil to get the chicken, the pan was empty. No carcass, no chicken pieces, nothing. Just an empty, greasy pan covered with foil. I started to cry because I thought, "This is it. I have finally sunk so low that I forgot that I ate dinner."

I opened up the garbage can and started digging around in it, trying to see through my tears if there were any chicken bones in there—proof that I had eaten but did not remember doing so. But there were no chicken parts of any kind in the trash. And then I remembered who I lived with... and I stopped crying.

Gun wasn't acting particularly guilty, but he never *looked* guilty about doing things he knew he wasn't supposed to do, because he never *felt* guilty. He would rather exercise his free will and live with the consequences. So, I demanded that he present his paws for inspection, and found grease all over his paw pads. He had eaten that entire chicken off the counter, bones and all, and re-covered the pan when he was done. But he hadn't been able to destroy the evidence on his paws. I don't know how he did it, but I have heard of other dogs performing similar stunts, even though they lack opposable thumbs. Their gluttony inspires them to rise to Houdini-like feats when it comes to food. And the cherry on the cake was that after I went to bed on an empty stomach, he had a long night of repeated bouts of diarrhea, so neither of us got any sleep. He was lucky, of course, because the chicken bones could have gotten stuck in his intestines and killed him. He was even luckier that I didn't kill him myself. As I said earlier, he would have been fine on his own, so long as someone provided food regularly, including whole chickens.

In many ways, living in Switzerland was not a good time for us and was not a good time for me personally, even if it was professionally rewarding. And it only got more difficult after Gunny's medical adventures began. Up until he ruptured one of his bicep tendons playing with Bacchus, Gun had seemed to be in good health. I must admit that he had often seemed grumpy, but it never occurred to me that he didn't feel well. I just assumed he was getting moody as he got older. I now know that was ridiculous — he was only seven years old for goodness sake — but I was naïve at the time.

In an effort to avoid surgery, we tried acupuncture and osteopathy to treat the tendon. Although those efforts failed, in the process we met two of the most wonderful people in the world — Dr. Piguet (a veterinary osteopath) and Dr. Stucki-Marmier (an acupuncturist). We all agreed that surgery was the only option, so we did the usual blood work before surgery to be sure everything was in order. It was, and the surgery was a success.

Shortly after Gunny recovered, we took the boys to a nearby forest on a beautiful fall Sunday to walk a twelve-mile trail that we loved. That morning, one of Gunny's gums was oozing a little blood, but I assumed he had just irritated it the night before while eating his Dentabone to clean his teeth. There wasn't a lot of blood and he otherwise seemed okay, so off we went.

I don't carry much guilt with regard to my relationship with Gunny because I honestly did the best I could for him at every turn. But on that day, I failed him by taking him on that hike. For much of the walk he seemed okay, but by the time we got to the end, he was so exhausted he lay down at the edge of the parking lot and could go no further. Juan Carlos had to drive the car across the parking lot to pick us up. He had had enough water and food, and he wasn't really limping, so there was no easy explanation—but that gum was still oozing.

I called the emergency vet number when we got home and did my best to explain to them in French what was happening with his gums. They said if they were pink that I didn't need to bring him in and we could wait to see the regular vet in the morning.

We took him to the doctor the next morning, and I am sorry to say that the vet seemed much more interested in watching Gunny walk to assess his surgical skill on his tendon than he was in his bleeding gum. He said it seemed odd that it was still bleeding, but perhaps he had cracked a tooth, so he gave me antibiotics and sent us home. Monday and Tuesday passed and he was still oozing blood from his gums. He was also very lethargic, although being Gunny, he was still eating. But I was getting panicky.

I called the vet on Wednesday morning and told him what was happening. He said, "I'm really busy today, do I really have to see him this afternoon?"

I said, "Well, you're the vet so you tell me, but it seems to me that if a dog is bleeding for three days straight and the medication has made no difference, he needs to see a doctor."

Juan Carlos took him to the vet that afternoon, and when the vet called me at 5 p.m., his tone was quite different.

"Mrs. Duperier, we have a big problem with your dog. He doesn't have enough platelets and is bleeding internally because he either ate rat poison, or he has cancer. I have called the specialty hospital at the University of Bern and they are expecting you. You must drive there as fast as you can."

Chapter 7

*['What was the best moment of my life?' you ask.]
For me there have been many moments, not just one,
like when you are walking along a rocky beach and
all of sudden one rock stands out from all the rest
and seems to sparkle in the sunlight even though it
isn't shiny up close. You could say it was wet from
the water lapping up against it so that is the reason
for your attraction or you could say the sun got in
your eyes and for a brief moment your vision was
impaired but for some reason you were able to see
that particular rock. That is what I believe my special
moments have been, little unexpected jewels.*

*But since I know you want me to talk about us,
Laurie, I will say I was delighted when I first knew
you finally loved me and we both realized we had a
special bond. If I was difficult or if I still am it's partly
because I have never been that thrilled with my dog
self. I don't like not having control over my life or the
limitations of the dog body. It's like I'm living in two
realities at the same time and never quite knowing
which one I'm going to experience at any particular
moment. I can be having a beautiful thought in my*

head, like a daydream, and then find myself eating
some disgusting dead thing because that other part
of myself found it interesting, bringing me out of my
special moment.

I haven't always been aware of my nature, which
changed when I almost died in Switzerland, and
as the years have passed I seem to be more aware of
my other self. I know that's another story but it also
touches on this subject. Actually I think I did die in
Switzerland for I was swept up into a hazy cloud and
was approached by people or beings in white.

Ganimedes

It is difficult, even now, for me to talk about what
happened to him Switzerland. This was not a situation in
which Gunny was ill and would need some time to recover.
This time, he was dying right before my very eyes. I could feel
him slipping away from me.

As the vet had instructed, we drove to Bern, which was
over an hour away from our house. It was a horrible night.
The fog was thick and there was a nonstop drizzle coming
down. When we finally found the hospital, it looked closed,
but someone came down to let us in when I rang the buzzer.

Gun walked into the hospital on his own power, but he
was very quiet. The vet in Bern told me that they had spoken
to the vet in Lausanne and knew the situation. The first thing
I said was, "He had a tick disease when we lived in Hong
Kong. Is it possible that that is what is causing this?"

The vet said, "No," in a very matter-of-fact tone of voice. "Go home and wait for a call in the morning." (I was a rookie back then. No one ever got me to leave a hospital so easily without Gunny again.)

Gunny's technical condition was "grave". A dog normally has between 175,000 and 450,000 platelets per microliter of blood. Platelets are essential in that they enable your blood to clot when you're bleeding, and keep you from spontaneously bleeding out. I don't know how many platelets Gunny had the previous Sunday, but it had to have been less than 50,000 or his gum wouldn't have bled like that. By Wednesday, when we got to the hospital, he had less than 20,000. He was black and blue all over from hemorrhaging under his skin, which they discovered when they shaved his foreleg to draw blood and put in an IV. It was painful to him to be touched, so they put him in a kennel that was literally padded all over for his comfort and to prevent even the slightest bump from causing another bleed.

We went to the hospital the next morning, Thursday, to discuss his condition and the proposed treatment. They had determined that in addition to having very few platelets, he was also anemic. This combination of problems, which is very dangerous, is called Evans syndrome. They did not know the cause of the problem, but they said it was likely immune mediated, meaning that his body was killing its own platelets and red blood cells. So, they needed to "turn off" his immune system to get it to stop trying to kill him. To do that, they pumped him full of massive doses of steroids and a drug called azathioprine, which carried a small risk of pancreatitis but was necessary. They also gave him human immunoglobulin to try to "trick" his immune system, and another drug to stimulate his bone marrow. Nothing worked.

I asked a few questions.

"Again, could this be a relapse of the tick disease from Hong Kong?"

Answer: "Unlikely."

"Did you give him platelets to help his blood clot?"

Answer: "No, we do not have dog platelets to transfuse."

"We must have dog platelets in the United States, so maybe I could ship some from there?"

Answer: "No, you don't have dog platelets in the United States. I studied at Louisiana State University, and I know. They do not exist."

In the end, they were wrong about all of it. I didn't know that at the time, but what I knew was that I wasn't going to stop trying to save Gunny.

The only reason I knew to ask about the platelets at all was because when I worked for one of those big law firms, I had represented the American Red Cross for years in their transfusion-associated AIDS cases. As you likely know, many people were infected with HIV from blood transfusions in the early '80s, and many of those people sued the blood banks. My job was to defend the Red Cross, and as a result, I knew quite a bit about blood products as compared to the average person. Platelets were not going to cure Gunny, but they could buy some time for us to fix the underlying problem by keeping him from bleeding to death while we were trying to figure things out. It just seemed illogical that dog platelets did not exist, when human blood banks had platelets for people. It would take a lot of donor dogs to make a bag of platelets, but it was possible.

When I arrived at the hospital on Friday morning, I was told that he was worse—he was down to five hundred platelets and they did not know why he had not yet bled into a major organ and died. They told me that he could literally die at any moment. The intern taking care of Gunny said to me, "Mrs. Duperier, you need to understand that your dog is not going home. He cannot live."

I said, "Anaise, you don't know me and you don't know my dog. He is coming home. So instead of sitting here and telling me that he is going to die, why don't you go talk to your colleagues and figure out how to save him?"

"I wish that it was possible to save him, but my textbook tells me otherwise."

Neither Gunny nor I had read her textbook and were not terribly interested in its prognostication. I just knew it was not his time.

After about thirty minutes, several doctors came out and said, "You mentioned that you have another dog in the car with you?"

I said, "Yes; Bacchus, our other Lab."

"Is there anything medically wrong with Bacchus?"

"Not that I know of."

"Then you should bring him into the hospital so that we can type his blood. If his blood type matches Gunny's, we can do a fresh whole-blood transfusion that would give Gunny some platelets, although not a lot."

Bacchus' blood was a match for Gunny's. Hoorah! We went with Bacchus to the back of the hospital to a small cold room with a steel examination table on it. He was scared, but did his best to stay calm. They lay Bacchus down on his side on the table and held him very firmly, then stuck a needle into his jugular vein so that they could get enough blood to transfuse to Gunny. I spoke softly in Bacchus' ear, "You are a good boy and I love you so much." When they were finished, I held the bag of blood in my hands, still warm from Bacchus' body, and told Bacchus that he was going to make magic for Gunny.

Bacchus' blood gave Gunny about ten thousand platelets. That was not enough to stop his internal bleeding, but it was more than the five hundred platelets he had. I know that Bacchus gave Gunny his blood with all of his love, and for twenty-four hours, his blood kept Gunny alive.

Chapter 8

[When I died in Switzerland], there was one man [among the beings in white who] was tall and had strong features. He came and asked me if I was willing to continue on my journey. He said it wouldn't be easy to continue living, but in the end I would have some important opportunities to evolve out of my present state. He said it wasn't for certain but it was an open-ended possibility, and that I was to learn about humility among many other things that I'm sure we will get to. Humility. Well I have learned that over and over again. I have not been one in the past who liked relinquishing control over my life or my body.

The man seemed to know many things about me. He said in the past I had been a natural leader but not always a deep thinker, and in this dog life I was to be given the opportunity to look at life and the human condition from many different perspectives because of you, Laurie, and the company that you keep. I obviously went along for the ride. That may have been my best moment because that is when everything changed and I knew not only did I have a choice but I became aware of my self, my consciousness, and have been getting clearer ever since. I realized that I do have a purpose that goes beyond just inhabiting this body called Gunny . . .

I guess it started in China, a place I couldn't call home and didn't fully understand. I could have left this body then and hoped for another life in another body. Did I survive in Switzerland because of the conscious choice I made to continue on this path with the aid of Laurie's resolve, or was it destiny?

Ganimedes

While Bacchus' blood gave Gunny's body some more platelets to kill, it could not save him. We were no closer to curing Gunny, but thanks to Bacchus, he was still alive.

The Friday afternoon of the blood transfusion, I did one of the most selfish things that I have ever done in my life—I told Gunny that he did not have permission to die. Period.

"It is not your time. You can't leave me here. You have to promise to give me five more years. Promise. I will make it worth your while. Just don't go. I know that you are so tired and this is so hard, but you can do this. We are doing everything possible. You just need to keep fighting and give us some time to fix what is wrong."

He was, after all, only seven years old. It was greedy and selfish on my part to say that to him. But I'm not sorry and I don't regret it.

The "we" I spoke to Gunny about had become quite a large group of people. Since the night that Gunny was admitted to the hospital, I had been calling friends all around the world and asking them to send their good thoughts and love to Gunny. I don't care if you are Buddhist, atheist, or Catholic—your religious beliefs have nothing to do with your ability to send loving thoughts and positive energy to someone in need. I would never have asked a bunch of people to stop what they were doing to pray for *me*, but without hesitation I asked them all to help Gunny. I had never done anything like that before, but I instinctively knew that medicine alone was not going to save him. He needed love and healing energy to help him fight.

The response from my friends and family was overwhelming. I had emails and phone calls from literally a hundred people, dubbed "Team Gunny", who said that they were praying for him and lighting candles for him across the globe—from butter candles at a Buddhist altar at home in Switzerland, to a candle in Saint Patrick's Cathedral in New York City—and also doing their best to think of him every single day. I spoke to Dr. Piguet and Dr. Stucki-Marmier, and they too assured me they were praying for him and sending him love.

Dr. Piguet's words are burned into my memory: "I know it is hard for you to see it when you are so scared and Gunny is so sick, but Gunny has brought together people from all around the world who don't even know each other to pray for him. I think that if you see it from above the earth, all of that beautiful energy, from all of those people, it looks like a rainbow." *Gunny's Rainbow*.

Unlike Dr. Piguet, the vets in Bern believed that Gunny was going to die. They had merely humored me by transfusing Bacchus' blood on Friday night. I later found out that they could have called for one of their donor dogs days earlier to donate fresh blood for Gunny, just like Bacchus had done, but they thought the situation was too hopeless to bother: "We believe that his bone marrow is dead and that he can no longer make platelets, which means that even if you could find platelets somewhere, it would not matter because he cannot make his own platelets going forward, and that is necessary in order for him to live."

I didn't believe his bone marrow was dead, and they had no way of knowing. I was determined to find some platelets to buy more time, but the clock was ticking.

Although I wasn't working, I spoke multiple times a day to my boss, Andy, who understood both the medical situation and my emotional state, as he loved his dog Teddy like I loved Gunny. Andy came to my rescue. He and his wife set about doing research on Gunny's condition to confirm that the hospital was doing all that it could, and they started looking for dog platelets in the United States — a friend had told me she was almost sure there were dog platelets in the US. Before it was all said and done, Andy had involved several senior vice presidents in my company in both Switzerland and New York in the quest to get Gunny platelets. They had located a blood bank in the Midwest that had frozen, shippable platelets, found a vet in New York to write a prescription for them, and arranged for the platelets to be shipped overnight to a friend's apartment in Manhattan. They also had arranged for a senior executive who was flying from New York to Switzerland on Saturday night to bring the platelets to Lausanne. This required my friend to find fresh dry ice in Manhattan in October to keep the platelets frozen on the trip, and to deliver the two carry-on ice coolers full of dog platelets to our colleague's hotel, along with a legal opinion that importation of dog platelets was legal under Swiss law, just in case he was stopped by Swiss customs on arrival.

Chapter 9

Team Gunny. How kind you all are, how thoughtful and enduring. When I have been ill or in perilous situations, Laurie has gathered you all together to send love and prayer to me. I have to admit I have not thought about it until now. But when I do, I cry because I didn't recognize how truly amazing that is. If I had not been so fortunate to meet so many amazing people I would not have a true perspective either. For many of you I cannot visualize a face, but I will try to look for you and kiss you one by one. I cry again. Why would you care for me? Is that what it is to be truly human? Is that my shortcoming? Why do I deserve this when so many others get nothing, nothing at all? You have so much light and love in you. There are so many of you [who] have changed me forever.

Ganimedes

The platelets arrived in Lausanne on Sunday morning, but it was too late. That morning, the chief resident at the hospital called me at home at 8 a.m. When I answered the phone and heard her voice, I literally dropped to my knees and stopped breathing. Not once in four days had anyone from Bern called me—mostly because there was no need—I called the hospital more or less every hour, day and night, to check on Gunny's condition when I wasn't sitting vigil in the hospital lobby. So when I heard Dr. Luchschandel's voice, I collapsed because I was sure she was calling to tell me that he was dead.

She said in perfect English, "Mrs. Duperier, I wanted to let you know that we tested his blood this morning and he is making platelets. Big. Fat. Juicy. Platelets. He has seventeen thousand of them, and I know that because I counted them myself. He doesn't need the platelets that you are bringing."

How was this possible, you ask? In a nutshell, the cause of his Evans syndrome was the Babesia parasite he had acquired from a tick in Hong Kong. We now know that the imidocarb they had given Gunny in Hong Kong, which is an effective treatment in about 95 percent of all cases, had not killed all of his parasites. As would be true for the rest of his life, Gunny was the outlier, the 5 percent.

It would appear that the few remaining parasites had lain dormant in his system for two years, likely the reason that he had not felt great and was grumpy. The surgery to release his bicep tendon had put stress on his immune system, which allowed the parasites to start multiplying again, attacking his body. Had they given Gunny the imidocarb on Wednesday when we got to the hospital, it would have saved him days of suffering. But they had not given it to him until Saturday, when they got blood test results that showed he had been exposed to babesia—which I had told them days earlier. Once he received the imidocarb, just like in Hong Kong, it began killing the parasites, and as the parasite load dropped, his body essentially came out of the flat spin that it had been in.

Obviously, his bone marrow was not dead. He was perfectly capable of making platelets. "Big. Fat. Juicy. Platelets." His bone marrow started producing them rapidly, and within days, his platelet levels had returned to normal. He came home two days later—seven days after he had been admitted to the hospital near death.

We never transfused the platelets to Gunny—I donated them to the hospital to save another dog. But the beautiful energy that all my coworkers created on his behalf, along with the love and prayers that Team Gunny had sent to him for days, had given him the strength to survive. I can assure you that for the week he was ill, dying would have been easier than surviving had been. But he chose to live. For all of the possibilities that had been put before him by the man in white. Because he felt all of the love from Team Gunny willing him on. And because Gunny and I now understood the power of our bond. For Gunny to have felt that the moment he chose to live, in the midst of his suffering, was the best moment of his life is, for me, extraordinary. It is also a master lesson in gratitude. He was grateful for the chance to live, grateful to have been given a choice, and grateful for everything that came later—even the bad times.

My telling him he did not have permission to go would not have stopped Gunny had he really wanted to give in; he never did anything just because I told him to do it. Rather, I believe that my asking him to fight, and letting him know that I was fighting right alongside him, as were lots of other people, awakened his warrior spirit.

"Warrior" can be defined in different ways. I recently read a description of a warrior in Paulo Coelho's book *Aleph* that instantly made me think of Gunny:

> [H]e believed in the impossible and, for that reason, won a battle that everyone . . . considered to be lost. That is what marks out the warrior: the knowledge that willpower and courage are not the same thing. Courage can attract fear and adulation, but willpower requires patience and commitment.

Gunny was many beautiful things, and at his core, he was a valiant but gentle warrior.

Good thing, because I am sorry to tell you that Gunny then developed life-threatening pancreatitis from the azathioprine about a week after he came home. He went back into the hospital, throwing up blood and in severe pain. The only treatment for pancreatitis was to give him fluids, fast him, and pray — again. It was horrible for him after having just been through so much. I brought him home five days later, the pancreatitis having more or less resolved. But it had all taken a horrible toll on him, both psychologically and physically.

Gunny looked horrible. He had lost one quarter of his body weight — twenty pounds — in those three weeks. He slept all day and did not have the energy to go for walks. He looked like a skeleton from all the steroids and was pretty much spent.

We went to see Dr. Stucki-Marmier for acupuncture, hoping it would help him recover. He was so exhausted that he just lay on the floor of her office, not moving much. She said to me, "I think that you need to consider giving him permission to go. He is so very tired, and he stays only for you. I think that you need to ask him what he wants to do."

I did not resent her for saying this to me. I had two perfectly good eyes in my head and I knew that he was struggling and exhausted. The Evans syndrome followed by the pancreatitis was just too much. I said to her, "I know that you are right, but I cannot give him that permission. It is not his time and he can't leave. I wish that I were a big enough person to let him go, but I'm not. He is the glue that holds our family together, and I don't know what will happen to us if he dies."

With compassion for both of us, she said, "That is a mighty big responsibility for a dog."

The thought of living without Gunny was unbearable to me. During his illness, we had clung to each other literally for dear life, and we did not know how to let go again. I can't say we really tried, though. Letting go of each other didn't hold much appeal for us.

I am not suggesting that it was okay to put my relationship with Gunny ahead of my relationship with everyone else, including Juan Carlos. It was not a reasoned decision. It wasn't even something that I consciously chose to do. It just was.

In the midst of all this drama with Gunny, my company transferred me again—this time back to Washington, D.C.

During our time in Switzerland, my ladder climbing had gone well—I had been promoted to vice president, heading the company's worldwide compliance department. The job I was offered in Washington was even bigger, and I was excited about the promotion. I loved my job, my boss, and my team in Switzerland. But living there had taken a toll on each of us as individuals and as a family. We needed to go *home*, or even Gunny's glue was not going to be able to hold us together.

Gunny was too weak to fly, however. So, I moved to Washington, and Juan Carlos took the boys to Spain for a few months for Gunny to regain his strength. Just one problem— now there was something very wrong with his liver. Where on earth was I going to find someone to fix *that*?

Chapter 10

Mark is a testament to how a doctor should be. He is diligent, striving for excellence in whatever he is doing. I now know that much can be achieved if one has an open mind and their ego is balanced. Desire is important but so are honesty, integrity, empathy, and an open mind. Mark has all these qualities and more, so I feel lucky that he cares enough to stretch his knowledge and imagination when it comes to me and all my peculiarities and problems.

I've come to totally trust him, which is big for me since before this life I trusted no one. I'm still working on that issue but find it interesting that Mark always talks to me man to man, not man to dog, so I've always felt like an equal when he is around. Dogs don't really have best friends other than the people in their family (if they're lucky), but Mark is a true friend to me. I know if we were both men now we could talk on any subject and might even enjoy going fishing together and sharing a drink. I can visualize us sitting back and discussing life and the Universe. Mark has also opened up my mind to the endless possibilities out there of ways to help others. I like how he thinks and

he surprises me sometimes with his humor. I admire
his endless compassion. He makes me question if I'm
ready to embrace all the qualities it takes to be a good
man, a great man. I also think he understands what
it is like to be a dog.

Ganimedes

"Mark" is *Dr.* Mark, veterinarian extraordinaire. He is an internal medicine specialist, with a focus on liver disease, located in Annapolis, Maryland. He had successfully treated one of my friend's dogs for a liver problem years earlier, and when I told her about Gunny's new problem she suggested that I contact him. I wrote him a letter, asking for his help.

Dear Dr. Mark,

My name is Laurie Duperier . . . I am seeking your assistance for my seven-year-old Labrador retriever "Gunny" (formal name Ganimedes) . . . Gunny is the light of my life. He is not an ordinary dog, much less an ordinary Labrador retriever (I have another one, and he is different). He is stubborn, smart, fairly manipulative, and the most loyal being I have ever met. As you will see from the information below and in the enclosed medical records, he has defied all odds to live and we are doing our best to help him keep fighting. He has always had a big appetite, and I am happy to report that especially with the prednisone, he is eating every chance he gets. He has the mischievous look back in his eyes, so we know that he is in relatively good spirits.

I understand that you have not seen my dog, and therefore you cannot definitively opine on his condition. I believe your input would be helpful in the decisions that we have to make about his treatment, so would appreciate your advice. When Gunny is able to travel to the United States, I would like to put him in your care. He is too weak to travel right now, but I am hopeful that he will be able to do so in the next four to six weeks . . .

I arrived in Washington last night and would very much appreciate the opportunity to speak with you as soon as possible. I think you are the best chance he has, so thanks in advance for your help.

Sincerely,
Laurie Duperier

He actually called!

"Mrs. Duperier, I got your letter. I do not usually treat dogs I have never met for people I don't know, but okay, I'll help you."

And so began our lifelong friendship with Mark. While he is an amazing doctor, and that is crucial, he is also an amazing person without whom our lives would be quite different. Among other things, Gunny probably would not have seen eight years old, much less fourteen.

Why did Mark respond to my letter all those years ago? In part, I think it is because I presented him with an interesting case. Mark loves puzzles, and I gave him the equivalent of a canine Rubik's Cube. It had to be more than that, though. I think it was what Gunny has identified as one of Mark's most beautiful qualities — his endless compassion. In this instance, it was probably compassion for me as much as Gunny. I was a woman who wanted to get "the light of her life" home from another country, and I think on a very human level, he wanted to help.

With Mark's long-distance help, Gunny made it back home to Washington, D.C., in February, 2005. He was seven years old when he returned home from his worldly adventures. We found a new house not far from our old one in Bethesda, and Gunny was able to go to the same old parks and see old friends. He was even reunited with Sam, his childhood friend. It broke my heart, though, when Sam's dad, who had spent countless nights watching the dogs play, asked "Is that Gunny?" when he first saw him at the park. His illness had taken a huge toll, and we had a long way to go for him to be well.

Gunny officially became Mark's patient, and Mark had his work cut out for him. In the medical world, Gunny was considered a "zebra". No disease presented in the usual way so that it could be easily diagnosed, and even once we knew what the problem was, Gunny rarely responded normally to conventional treatments. Many of his diseases could have, and arguably should have, ended his life. They did, however, result in his having the biggest medical file in Mark's practice.

Let's begin with the fact that Mark did not assume that all of the babesia parasites from the Hong Kong tick were, in fact, dead. He suspected that they were just hiding, much like they had been after we moved from Hong Kong, waiting for an opportune moment to try to kill Gunny again. Blood tests revealed that Mark was right. But if the imidocarb had not killed them the first two times, what could we do? Mark scoured the veterinary literature to find a new drug therapy to end the life of those parasites once and for all. And later blood tests proved that finally, after all those years, we killed the beast.

It was Gunny's liver disease that had brought us to Mark in the first place, which turned out to be auto-immune chronic active hepatitis and cirrhosis of the liver — a rare, treatable, but often fatal, liver disease. There is no cure. Mark prescribed a drug cocktail to suppress Gunny's immune system, in order to get it to stop trying to kill his liver. Lucky for us, Mark was an expert at diagnosing and treating this disease, and as a result, Gunny lived for over seven years with it, longer than any other dog Mark had known. (And as crazy as it sounds, years later, my mother developed and almost died from the same disease because her doctors were not as smart as Mark, and did not diagnose it quickly.)

One day, years later, Gunny fell down on the ground in the park behind our house and couldn't stand up again. After trying unsuccessfully to get him up for an hour, I carried all 80 pounds of him home, and called Mark. When he x-rayed

Gunny, he found that he had horrific arthritis in his elbows and was in a lot of pain. Gunny had not limped one day of his life on those front legs, but as it turned out, that was only because they hurt *equally* badly, so it didn't do any good to put more weight on one leg than another. He was born with the defect that caused that problem, and there weren't a lot of good alternatives for treating it. Mark suggested a new possibility, stem cell therapy, and sent me to the only place in town that was doing stem cell injections at the time—it was there we met Dr. Peter. Because of that elbow problem, we assembled a veterinary Team Gunny that worked together for the rest of Gunny's life to achieve amazing results, over and over again.

Gunny was not afraid of his vets. He loved them. We needed them in order to stay together in this life; without them, he would have died many times over. They all met Gunny's criteria for being a good vet: *"Compassion and knowledge, but if you don't have a caring heart, find some other kind of work."* They all cared very deeply about him and about our family.

In addition to Mark, who was the team captain, there was Carol, Gunny's holistic/homeopathic vet. Gunny loved Carol because, *"she likes to try new things and is so caring. She has helped me a lot and I am grateful for that. Carol has a strength about her. She reminds me of a little girl with a big brain and a big heart even though I know she is a woman."*

Peter was his orthopedic surgeon/specialist. Gunny felt that he owed him a great debt for how he had helped him, but he also made it clear that he was jealous of Peter because he was married to Faith.

Faith was Gunny's rehabilitation vet, Peter's wife, and Gunny's "girlfriend" (at least in Gunny's mind), who made him swoon like a schoolboy.

Everyone makes fun of the fact that I think Faith is beautiful. She is, and is so kind to me. I don't really understand why Faith goes out of her way for me when she has such a big family at home, but it makes me think that maybe she finds me a little special. Her presence has the ability to make me feel quiet, in anticipation of something I can't quite put my finger on.

Arguably the craziest thing of all happened next. After we fixed his elbows, Gunny was limping badly on his left front leg and none of the vets knew why. Dr. Peter concluded that the pain was in Gunny's shoulder, and believed there were two possibilities—a rotator cuff injury or a nerve tumor that was causing pain. So he convinced me to stick him in an MRI machine, which terrified me both because he had to be anesthetized and because I was not interested in finding out that Gunny had cancer. In one of her many acts of kindness, Dr. Faith went with us to the MRI clinic so that she could be with Gunny when he went to sleep and could be the first person he saw when he woke up. In return, Gunny gave her a big bouquet of two dozen yellow roses to show his appreciation, along with a kiss.

I was a basket case while he was in the MRI machine. I felt like I couldn't breathe, waiting to hear the news. After a couple of hours, I went back to the recovery room where Faith and Gunny were. I knew from the look on her face that it was bad news. "There is nothing wrong with Gunny's shoulder. But he has a tumor in his thyroid gland and we have to assume that it's cancer. You need to take him to see Mark."

"Huh?" That's what his *vets* said, not me. They did, however, sit gape-mouthed when they recalled the recent aura drawing Alexandra had done depicting bright red energy in his neck, precisely where his thyroid gland was located. We don't know why a tumor in his thyroid gland made Gunny limp. For all I know, Gunny started limping so that someone would put him in an MRI machine, find the tumor, and cut it out. You pretty much *never* find thyroid cancer in a dog before it has spread. It just quietly grows and then kills them. Thus, the surgeon who removed the cancerous part of Gunny's thyroid told me that we should not expect him to live more than eighteen more months due to the deadly nature of that cancer. Gunny lived a lot longer than that, without any trace of thyroid cancer again.

Last but not least, there was the adrenal gland tumor we found when Gunny was thirteen years old, which on second thought, was probably weirder than the thyroid cancer. When Mark found the tumor on a routine ultrasound, it was pretty big. We considered what to do about it, and concluded that we would just watch it for a while and see if it got bigger, or if he started having any symptoms. (Neither Gunny nor I were interested in him having surgery again.) We waited a couple of months, and it grew a little. So we waited another couple of months, and when Mark tried to find it with the ultrasound, there was nothing but a normal adrenal gland to be found. The tumor had disappeared. Poof! Gone without a trace! Not once in thirty years of practice had Mark seen an adrenal tumor disappear. That's just how things went with Gunny.

The unusual nature of Gunny's problems pushed all of his vets to be better, more innovative doctors, and they achieved more with him than I think any of them ever thought possible because they worked as a team—and because Gunny had an extraordinary will to live. I can't tell you exactly how Gunny changed each one of them as people and as vets, but I know that he did.

For Faith, I think knowing Gunny reaffirmed what she already believed—that animals understand so much more than most people think, and that they want to be consulted and reassured about medical treatment the same way any human patient would. She talks to all the dogs she treats now, and they understand she is trying to help them. Everybody loves Dr. Faith.

In Mark's case, I think spending time with Gunny through the years awakened a different sort of spirituality in him—confirmation that there is more out there than conventional wisdom teaches us or can be easily explained. After all, being Gunny's doctor gave him the chance to repeatedly witness that almost anything was possible. In the last few years of Gunny's life, Mark sometimes heard Gunny talking to him, often late at night—and he in turn would talk to Gunny, especially when Gunny was ill and scared. Mark's voice reassured Gun in a way no one else's could because he loved and trusted Mark so much. One night when Mark had discharged us from the emergency room, feeling that Gunny was stable, Gunny kept trying to get back into the hospital, where Mark was, and basically refused to leave. He knew that he was ill, and was worried about what would happen to him if he left Uncle Mark. I finally just picked him up and put him in the car so we could go, and called Mark on the way home to ask him to talk to Gun to let him know he did not need to stay at the hospital, that he would be safe at home. Only after Mark spoke to him did Gunny start to relax.

Mark has since told me that he would not be the same vet—or person—if he had never met Gunny; and he was pretty awesome before we met him. But I know it would make Gunny happy and proud to feel that he contributed positively to Mark's life in some way. Everyone on the team, including me, enhanced Gunny's *quality* of life. But Gunny knew that it was Mark who enabled him to live.

Chapter 11

I think Laurie needed to slow down and do something different, more meaningful to her. In her lawyer days she was gone so much of the time and really didn't have much of a life of her own. I missed her so much when she was gone. Sometimes, like a child, I wondered if I was forgotten, still loved.

I do know how much Laurie loves me. She is my best friend because we have a connection, a history. Our life, this life, is intertwined. We have shared so much together. I am closer to Laurie than to any other human I know. She is my best love, the one who loves me no matter what, the one who is there for me, on call twenty-four hours a day. Who could be better, best than that? She feels so much for me it is really overwhelming sometimes because I don't know how I could ever pay her back. I know my love for her is deep and enduring, but I am so different than she. I don't know if I were human that I would be to her what she is to me.

Ganimedes

Have you ever watched a friend struggling to find the right direction in life and silently mused to yourself, "What *she* needs is a good whack upside the head!"? Well, I suppose that is what Gunny had been thinking about me. I don't think he felt I was doing a whole lot of good for the world in my legal job, and he didn't think my legal job was doing much good for me. While he would never have wished for harm to come to me, I was in fact whacked upside the head. I don't mean metaphorically whacked, like an "ah-ha" moment. I mean a *for real* whack upside the head with a four-by-six wooden beam. Even I have to recognize that a two-by-four might not have been strong enough to do the trick.

Sunday was my most peaceful day of the week. I had a routine. Go to yoga at 10:30 a.m. Stop by the sandwich shop after class. Eat lunch on my patio and read the Sunday *Washington Post*. Then lie in my wooden hammock under the big wild cherry tree in my backyard and alternate between continuing to read the *Post* and napping. On one particular Sunday, my routine took an unexpected turn. I lay down in the hammock, opened up the Style section, and heard a crack. The next thing I knew I was regaining consciousness on the ground under the cherry tree, blood gushing out of my head. The hammock had broken at the base, and the long wooden beam of the hammock stand, from which the hammock hung, had collapsed inward and catapulted into my head. It missed my eye by less than an inch and it took twenty-five internal and external stitches to close the wound on my forehead. Until that moment, I had never really contemplated the possibility that I could die in my backyard while reading the *Washington Post*. This put a new wrinkle in things.

My job in Washington was hard; long hours, some challenging personalities, and difficult legal issues. It was a big job, the kind of job I had been dreaming of my whole life: vice president and associate general counsel of a Fortune 10 company. I worked across several time zones on urgent issues, and it seemed the day always started at 7 a.m. and didn't end until the last phone call from the West Coast at 10 p.m. There had been so many years of so much hard work and such long hours. For what? I was starting to have trouble remembering why exactly I was doing this. The money was amazing, but I had never been someone motivated primarily by money. I had had passion about my work and enjoyed my jobs, but now my passion was waning and I was feeling worn out.

I needed something more. I needed to feel like what I did mattered. I needed to know that I was living my life, not just marking time. I wanted to do some good in the world. And if I thought I had a few years to figure it all out, that illusion was shattered on a Sunday afternoon in September in my own backyard. The question I kept repeating to myself was, "How long am I going to wait to start living my life?"

The answer was, "Not long." About the time I was whacked in the head, my company was working on breaking itself up into several parts. This provided several opportunities for me. I could go back to Switzerland, stay in D.C. doing a modified version of my current job, or leave the company. I had worked with fabulous people and had had a really wonderful career. There was nothing material that I needed or wanted and didn't have. But what I really wanted more than anything, was to have *time*, and most especially, time to be with Gunny. He was ten years old now, and for so much of his life, I had lived on the road. I just wanted to be with *him*.

In the two-and-a-half years since we had returned from Switzerland, he had faced more health challenges — you saw the list — and needed more and more help. He was having trouble walking up and down stairs and required lots of different medications and monitoring to keep his liver functioning. I was a good lawyer and had achieved a lot. But the thing that brought me the most gratification and happiness was taking care of Gunny. I knew that I was *really* good at that.

I spoke to Mark about the possibility that I would leave my job, and told him that I would like to find a job helping animals — maybe a non-profit dedicated to animal welfare, something along those lines. He told me that what was really needed in the D.C. area were more dog swimming pools because there was a big need and few pools. And, he told me that given the condition of Gunny's spine and joints, he really needed to swim in order to maintain his mobility. I was all for taking Gunny to swimming lessons. But I laughed out loud at the notion that I would build a dog pool.

"Oh my goodness no, Mark, I'm not thinking of opening a business or anything like that. I'm trying to relax and quasi-retire."

I called the few pools in the area to make an appointment for Gunny to swim, but no one would accept him! Gunny could not be vaccinated because of the autoimmune diseases he had, and no one would let him swim without vaccinations, even though his blood tests showed he had immunity to all the usual communicable diseases. This was a stupid policy, and a real problem for us because he was getting weaker and weaker in his right hind leg and I knew he was losing his ability to walk.

I don't know what to say except that I considered it all a sign from the Universe that I should quit my job and open a dog pool. I don't have a better explanation than that. Abandoning my chosen profession in my early forties, at the height of my career, was not an easy decision, but it felt wrong to continue on the path that I was on. It would make a better story to tell you that I gave it all up for Gunny, but that is only partially true. He was a big factor in my decision-making, but the bottom line was, I quit for me. I had lost my passion for my job, but my passion for helping Gunny, and our bond, was stronger than ever.

Juan Carlos and I agreed that we would not return to Switzerland (I didn't want to live there and I could not take Gunny away from his vets), nor would I look for another local legal job. I would take the company exit package and quit practicing law. *To build a dog pool.* And where was I going to put this indoor dog swimming pool? We concluded that the only way to do this was for us to move out of our very comfortable new house and buy a house with enough land to build an indoor pool for dogs to swim in, which would be called Gunny's Rainbow, of course.

Chapter 12

When I first heard about the pool, I was excited. It sounded like a good idea, but then we moved. I wasn't thrilled about that. I was comfortable in our other house. Bacchus and I had a lot of fun there. We enjoyed our routine, our walks particularly with Juan Carlos, and the yard. Even though it wasn't large, it was pleasant and inviting to sit outside. We liked when we had company. It was easy and comfortable.

Then we moved and little by little all hell broke loose. I worried our family would burst apart like a balloon exploding. We got through it somehow but it wasn't pleasant. For a while I associated everything going wrong [in life] with the pool construction and the unpleasant workers going in and out, the unending noise, the weird goings on, the ghosts, and too many unfamiliar sounds and smells. It wasn't always the ghosts that frightened me, sometimes it was the sounds I would hear. The creaking and groaning of some of the trees, voices in the wind, the sound of horses' hooves, and the screams and cries. Sometimes the house reeked of anxiety.

There have been many ghosts at our home. Some frightening, some interesting. I didn't want to be left alone with them. I felt vulnerable because my body has been weakened with age and disease. I didn't think I could fight back. I also knew they didn't belong here. That was one of my worst experiences, not them as much as the fear I couldn't protect myself, my family. As I've said before, I hate feeling vulnerable.

Ganimedes

Honestly, I dreaded writing this chapter because if you are on board with the fact that my dog talks like a philosopher through my clairvoyant friend, now I have to ask you to wrap your mind around the fact that we accidentally bought a haunted house. Okay. Here goes.

Do I believe in ghosts? I do now. I don't know what I believed before I moved to this house. I suppose I thought it was possible, like anything is possible, but I didn't really give it much thought. I figured that most alleged ghost sightings had a logical non-ghost explanation. Do I see ghosts? Not really. I saw one once, but it was such a fleeting second that I'm not sure if I made it up.

I *can* tell you this—I did not have a bad feeling when I found the place for the pool, and I did not sense that anything was amiss. In fact, it was quite the opposite. I had searched for at least six months for the right place to build Gunny's Rainbow, hoping to find a quiet place where the dogs who came to swim would be able to relax, have fun, absorb love, and heal. When I found a great piece of land in the middle of Bethesda, Maryland, surrounded by beautiful century-old oaks and other magnificent trees, I literally jumped up and down because I just *knew* this was it. This was where I was supposed to build Gunny's Rainbow. So, far from having a bad feeling about the place, my intuition told me that it was the perfect place. As a result, we didn't negotiate very hard and I paid a hefty price for the land.

The existing house on the property could best be described as a shack. It had been more or less abandoned for five years, so the chipmunks, squirrels, rats, and rabbits were the current tenants. There was no grass *anywhere*, just enormous overgrown azaleas and rhododendrons in the front yard, and waist-high weeds in the back. (This was most upsetting to Gunny, by the way, because grass was so very important to him.) There was a rotting picket fence in the front yard that made it impossible to see that there even *was* a house under the overgrown shrubs. Last but not least, there were about a hundred and fifty saplings growing on the street side of that fence—apparently each time a squirrel had dropped a nut during the previous fifty years, a tree had sprouted. In other words, the place was a dump. A giant eyesore sitting in the middle of one of the wealthiest neighborhoods in the area. And this eyesore was all ours, including the magnificent lot with fifty majestic old-growth trees.

The plan was to move into the shack, put most of our furniture into storage, get the pool built so that Gunny could start swimming, and then begin the process of expanding and renovating the house. This was supposed to take about nine months to a year. If you have ever renovated a house, you are rolling on the floor laughing right now at this time estimate. I had never renovated a house before. I didn't laugh then, and I'm not laughing now.

The house had been built in about 1942, and the original owners lived in it until their death. The husband died last, about seven years earlier. One of the neighbors told us that he had died in the house and that it "took a while" for him to be found. Oh. Well, that might explain the rather strange smell that occasionally seemed to be wafting about the house.

Gunny was unhappy from the moment we moved in. My buddy, the one who was attached to me at the hip and was never more than five feet away from me, tried to run away in the first week. Even though he couldn't exactly run at that point, he was high-tailing it as fast as he could through the woods behind the house, with me running behind shouting *stop*, trying to catch him. I finally tackled him and we both went crashing to the ground, thankfully unharmed. What on earth was going on?

Gunny also routinely refused to come back in the house after going for a walk. He either took off down the street or ran across it into the neighbor's backyard, all in order to avoid coming home. I would often have to drag him up the driveway against his will to get him back in the house. Then, the panic attacks started. He would go down into the basement, crawl under Juan Carlos' desk, and tremble. I couldn't get him to come out for hours at a time. Nothing like this had ever happened in any other place that we'd lived, and I was worried about him.

I took him to see Mark a couple of times, even to the

emergency room once when he was having a panic attack, but no one could find a medical reason for his behavior. So I called Alexandra. She told me matter-of-factly that the old man who had lived in the house was "still here" and that was what was scaring Gunny. But it didn't stop there—she also saw several Native American spirits, including an older man on a horse whom we dubbed "the Chief", a young woman, and also a young man who seemed pretty mean. There were sometimes other Native American spirits around on horseback, but these three were the main characters. Apparently Gunny could see and hear them—it was probably the first time in his life that he had seen ghosts—and he was scared. (I don't know what Bacchus saw or heard, but he gave no indication that he was bothered in any way. He just wanted me to throw the ball and rub his tummy while his brother flipped out in the basement.)

On a bitterly cold morning four months after we had moved into our new house, the earthmovers rolled in to begin construction on the pool room. At the same time, Alexandra, an old friend from Los Angeles named Sharon, and I stood outside in the backyard of my fabulous new property and tried to figure out what to do about the spirit situation. Sharon is not clairvoyant in the same way that Alexandra is, but she is very intuitive. We agreed that we would all take ten minutes to see what we "picked up", and then huddle and compare notes. Sharon went to one side of the property and Alexandra to the other. They stood there quietly, concentrating intensely. I took the opportunity to contemplate my navel, because I can assure you, I didn't see or hear diddle. I was very cold, and was starting to doubt our sanity.

Sharon walked over to me and said, "A Native American girl was raped and murdered in your backyard, but I don't think she is buried here. The murderer was a young Native American." Then Alexandra came over and said that the Chief had shown her the whole thing like a movie: his daughter had been raped and murdered by a young man from a different tribe, and they had all essentially been stuck here and locked into this never-ending drama for the past several hundred years or so. And let's not forget the ghost of the prior owner, a nice old man who loved his house, didn't want to leave it, and was a little lost.

We did our best to encourage them all to move on—we burned frankincense and sent them Reiki, a healing energy, to help them transition to their next stop. Nothing happened. No one seemed to leave. The one time I thought I saw a ghost, it was the old man—for a split second, I saw this hunched-over, gaunt old man walk past the window of the house. I still don't say his name because for so long we just referred to him as "He Who Shall Not Be Named" (like Lord Voldemort in the *Harry Potter* series), lest speaking his name should rouse him.

While I think the old man's presence annoyed Gunny, I felt it was the Native American spirits who really caused him stress—their history was much less benign. I regularly went through the house with a smudge stick—a collection of sage and other herbs—to shoo them out and get rid of any negative energy. Gunny didn't have a panic attack every day, but when he did, I would sternly tell anyone who was listening to get out of the house and leave us alone.

At one point, I actually made a sign in big black Sharpie that said, "IF YOU ARE DEAD AND YOU'RE READING THIS, STAY OUT OF MY HOUSE. YOU SCARE MY DOG." I taped it to the window of the back door. I promise you that for the two weeks Juan Carlos tolerated that sign hanging on the door, Gunny did not have one single panic attack.

While all this was going on, we continued construction on the pool and the new garage. It took eight months or so to finish—the same amount of time that renovating the whole house was supposed to take. As Gunny told you, the construction was miserable. Indescribably miserable. And while all construction is bad, we had a series of events that read a lot like Gunny's list of illnesses—any one of them could have killed us but somehow didn't. Or at least they should have driven us from the property, shrieking, with our hair on fire.

Fire. Did I say fire? Why yes, I did. There were two of them—one was started courtesy of Pepco, the electric company, by a faulty "heavy up" of power to the house. Within twenty-four hours of their fine work, we lost power. When they opened up the electric box to look for the problem, all the wiring inside had melted. A faulty connection had caused the electricity to arc for the previous twenty-four hours, and the only unanswered question in anyone's mind, which a Pepco employee actually verbalized, was, "I wonder why the house didn't burn down?"

The second fire happened after a freak summer storm blew through, with downdraft/tornado winds that roared down our street, mostly in front of our house. The giant old tree across the street fell onto our property, taking down the power lines and shearing in half a one-hundred and twenty year old oak on my property, before coming to rest on a smaller oak in front of the pool room. The top of the fallen tree was dangling over the house, poised to crash through at any moment if the small oak gave way. It was hard to focus on that impending doom, however, given the giant fire raging in the front yard and in the street from the downed power lines. The power lines had caught fire and ignited the fallen tree branches, and the flames coming out of the power lines in the street were so hot that they turned the cement curb into glass.

Did I mention that I was also declared a public health hazard? When we bought the house, the real estate agent (who also owned the property) had checked the box on the legal disclosure form indicating that the house was on public sewer; not a shocking disclosure here in the middle of the city. But when I brought my construction plans down to the County to get a building permit, they told me I could not add on to the house as long as I had that septic tank. *What septic tank?* Turns out, the old man had never put the house on public sewer, so if I wanted to build on the land, it was going to cost me about $35,000 to connect to public sewer. But first we had to find the septic tank.

After hours of digging up the backyard with a backhoe, we finally found it—in about the same spot where Alexandra and Sharon thought the Native American girl had been murdered. The top had rusted off the septic tank and it was partially patched with a piece of plywood, rendering the tank unstable. According to the inspector, not only might the "contents" seep out, that whole section of the backyard was at risk of cratering. The County suggested that I rope off the area *to be sure that my dogs didn't get sucked down into the septic tank*. I would just like to say that I had been called a variety of things in my legal career, but I had never been called a public health hazard until then.

Last but not least, amid all the struggles with the incompetent, overpriced, lying contractors, an image of a skull appeared in the stucco in between the two new garage doors. No mistaking what it was. We painted over it, but I know it is still there, and it creeps me out to this day.

Now, you probably thought when this chapter started that it would be hard for you to believe that I had ghosts and spirits wandering around the property. Little did you know that the construction process to build Gunny's pool would be far more unbelievable. The two things are related, though, I have no doubt. All the negative energy of the spirits on my land poisoned everything. I was depressed and angry. If building this pool to help Gunny and other dogs was supposed to be my path, my true calling, why had everything gone so horribly wrong? My old job of flying around first class, staying in swank hotels, eating fabulous meals, and making heaps of money was starting to look pretty good again. But it was too late. I had quit my job and this was my life.

Oh, and when the pool was finally finished, Gunny made it abundantly clear that he really, really hated to swim.

"The pool. The bane of my existence," he said.

Chapter 13

Laurie is really good at swimming the dogs. I know the pool was for me, but in the end it is for her. And Bacchus loves to swim. I like talking to the dogs that come to swim. I like to tell them Laurie will help them. She will find a way to communicate what is needed to their people, how to help their pain and suffering. She will help make them strong.

I have been so fortunate to have had a great life with love and understanding and have never wanted for a thing. When I think of all the dogs that have come to the pool or that I have seen at the vet's office or on the street who haven't been as fortunate, I seethe inside. I can usually recognize with just a glance if a dog passing by has been abused or nurtured. When I think of a fine dog like Max, and what he went through and how he survived, I wonder if there is even a possibility that people can evolve. I am frustrated when I think about this, but grateful I now know the truth. I am finally grateful to have had this experience [of life as a dog].

The gift of the pool to me has not been the swimming but the opportunity to communicate with the dying and the dead. To experience these fellow canine travelers who have left this earth. Each acquaintance has answered a question of what happens after and what it is like during. I don't want to be a ghost. I don't want to wander or lose my way. I want to earn my wings. I want to be an angel and if I return here to earth, I want to honor all living creatures by helping them to experience what I have.

Ganimedes

I opened Gunny's Rainbow a year after we had moved in to the new house, when Gunny was eleven years old. We were exhausted from the construction and couldn't take any more chaos, so we resigned ourselves to living in the shack as it was, and I turned my focus to getting my business off the ground and keeping Gunny on his feet.

In addition to having to build the pool, make a website, print brochures, contact vets, and so on, I also took courses to ensure that I had the proper training. As I learned, there are a lot of things you can do with a dog in a pool besides swim, and a lot of what you do is not obvious until you look at it from the dog's perspective—like giving them a place to stand in the pool so that they feel secure with all four feet on the ground while they rest in the water.

Some dogs are great swimmers and love to retrieve, like Bacchus. He was always ready to swim, any time, day or night. "*I love Laurie. She is beautiful! I love when she lets me swim and gives me treats. It is our special time together."* Thank you, Bacchus. I love you, too.

Other dogs are not so confident, even if they love water. Or, even if they were confident swimmers when they were young, when they become old, arthritic, or have other orthopedic problems, they don't feel so sure about their bodies anymore. These dogs, like Gunny, are my calling. In addition to supporting them while they swim, I massage them while they rest and let them float peacefully in my arms in the warm water. I have had magical moments in the pool with some of the elderly dogs who come to swim, and had hoped for such moments with Gun.

He would have none of it. I tried everything to please him—food, toys, life jackets—but it didn't matter. He was pissed off every time he had to get in the water. I know he felt unsure, but geez, I was the person who always took care of him—it's not like I was going to let him drown. He would not relent. Yet, he almost always felt better after swimming, and when he came out of the water, he hopped around like a puppy again for a little while. So, I made him swim once or twice a week to help with his arthritis and to give him a little non-impact exercise to maintain his strength, like it or not.

His time in the water was split between doing a few laps while I supported him, and standing on the bench in the pool eating chicken breast. Eating chicken took up the majority of the time, however. Well, that and me singing to him. I can't sing at all. It is actually painful to listen to. When Juan Carlos first met me and I was singing something softly in the car one day he said, "What did you do with the money that your parents gave you for singing lessons?" Mysteriously, this is considered humor in Spain. In retrospect, I do wonder if Gun might have been more willing to swim if I had stopped singing. Oh well. I will never know.

I will say this—the pool room, much like a shower, seemed to improve how I sounded. My usual tunes were, *You Are My Sunshine* (you know the words), and *You Are My Only One*, by James Taylor.

> *And you are my only one, you are my only one*
> *Don't be leaving me now, now you're my only one*
> *You are my only one*
> *You are my only one*
> *Well, I'm telling you now, now you're my only one*

Have I Told You Lately That I Love You? by Van Morrison was also on the play list.

> *Have I told you lately that I love you?*
> *Have I told you there's no one else above you?*
> *Fill my heart with gladness, take away all my*
> *   sadness,*
> *Ease my troubles, that's what you do.*

I also made up a silly song: "Don't tell anybody that my Mommy can't sing, my Mommy can't sing, my Mommy can't sing. Don't tell anybody that my Mommy can't sing, or sheeee woooon't siiiiing toooo meeeee!"

For years, I sang all these different songs to Gun when he was in the water. But I have to tell you, until I saw the James Taylor and Van Morrison lyrics in print on this page, I had not consciously processed what I was saying to him. The words had just come to me because he was *The One*. My only one. And he truly did fill my heart with gladness and did take away all my sadness.

Luckily for my dog clients, I do not sing to them. But I do talk to them, as did Gun. Most dogs come once or twice a week to swim, so Gun got to know some of the dogs fairly well. Once he started talking to the dogs at the pool, he seemed to understand that there were dogs who were worse off than he was, and apparently some of them continued to talk to him after they died. He considered himself to be the pool boss, notwithstanding his dislike of swimming, and he liked being a part of helping them. Max, Winston, and Diva were his favorites, and they were some of my favorites, too. Here is what he had to say about them:

Max, a yellow Lab who swam for multiple orthopedic problems but primarily to try to hold in place a permanently dislocated left hip –

Max is a very strong male soul. I say that because I see him now even though he passed away. He said he would be there for me. He intimidated me sometimes, but he is good to the core, a fellow warrior. He would talk to me sometimes about how fortunate I was to have grown up with Laurie. He holds Laurie in the highest esteem. He said he had been beaten many

91

times and almost starved to death. He was thrown out of a moving car. If he hadn't been lucky enough to meet Diana he might have held a grudge against human beings, especially men. I see he is a gentleman through and through. He would fight to the death for someone he loved but he wouldn't harm anyone ever without being provoked. He wants to thank Laurie for all she did for him and tried to do. He understands her plight in regards to me. He wanted to take her pain away. He could feel it when she held him.

Winston, a chocolate Lab who had several problems, but mostly a sore neck and weakness in his hind end —

Winston is gone now. He has been coming to the pool in spirit less and less now. I always know when he is going to show up because everything gets very quiet and still. Then there is a pause and he appears, lights up the room with his smile. He is very different than he used to be. He makes me think and wonder what happened after he left his physical body. He never talks. I know by looking at him it was something good. He seems peaceful. He told me that he will light my way when I leave. I thank him for that. I am fortunate to have him as a friend.

Diva, a black Lab who had survived cancer and was having difficulty walking at fifteen years old –

Diva is stoic and elegant. She has suffered physically a lot like I have. She is fortunate like I am to have been befriended by really good people who do everything in their power to keep her healthy and happy and loved. There are so many dogs who have not been loved. Diva and I are aware of that fact and we both thank our lucky stars and look in wonder at the people we have met along the way that love animals and do their best for them.

I never imagined that the pool's gift to Gunny would be helping him to understand how lucky he was to have a loving family, how normal it was to get old and have your body parts not work so well anymore, and how eventually everyone dies. I just thought I was going to help him maintain his mobility. I did not aim nearly high enough in terms of how Gunny would benefit from the pool.

That said, Gunny never gave me one good moment with him in the water. I came to understand, however, that it was a strategy. I think he knew it would be almost impossible for me to continue to work in the water after he died if I was haunted by beautiful memories of being in the water with *him*. I'm not suggesting that he secretly loved to swim, but I do think he was very proud of the work I did with the dogs and that it was important to him for me to continue to help others after he died. And he wasn't so sure I would be able to continue doing that if I was always thinking about him when I worked.

I think he was probably right, by the way.

Chapter 14

It's only looking back that my life makes sense. My purpose has unfolded little by little through the years but has only made an impact since I became aware of who I was in the past and [realized] I had a choice to do something about it, to pay my debt. Even still, I had often been lazy and done nothing, but getting older and realizing time is running out made me take advantage of my situation.

Something did change in the last couple of years. I became more observant of others and my need to fulfill my destiny became apparent. I don't want this chance to slip by. Why? I do not know for sure, but Laurie had a lot to do with it. Not many have had the opportunities I have. I think if it were not for all my trials and tribulations with physical issues I would still be floundering. It has often been unpleasant but always enlightening.

Juan Carlos has been a good friend, a great friend. He has done a lot for me and with me. When I was younger, we had a lot of fun. No one was better to play with than Juan Carlos. No matter where we went it was good to be with him. I miss our good times. I liked to run with him and have nice memories of the beach and trails we walked together. When Bacchus came along I worried he'd like him better and wouldn't play with me. But he still gave me my share of his time until I wasn't able.

I think it is hard for Juan Carlos not to be able to [go on long walks and play games] with me anymore because that is his nature. That is what makes him Juan Carlos and I worry he would be most unhappy if he were in my position as an old man, meaning not able to be physically active and carefree. I guess in my most humble moments I've wished to take that possibility from him, like a parent for his child, asking God to give me the affliction not my child. I don't know why I feel that way about Juan Carlos because I'm usually more selfish than that but I sincerely do. What we share now is this — we are both dreamers and want to share what we are good at with others, want to make an impression on others, which is why I began talking to the vets and other dogs.

Ganimedes

I don't know if you have ever been a caregiver for someone who is old or ill, or been old or ill yourself, but I would agree with Gunny that sickness and aging are "*often unpleasant but always enlightening.*" When we thought things couldn't get harder, they did. When we thought we couldn't take any more, we could. When we wondered whether it was worth it, whether we were doing the right thing by continuing to fight on, we had moments of such immense joy and love that we knew we wanted to keep fighting, knowing there would be more joy and love despite it all. *"Life is precious,"* as Gunny said. His deteriorating physical condition was hard on all of us at times, no one more so than him, but it never occurred to any of us to give in. We were having too much fun being together.

As time wore on, Gunny had more and more trouble getting around. It started with his being unable to get up and down stairs on his own. He responded well to acupuncture and was better for a while. When that wasn't enough, we started using a sling to help him up and down the stairs, but eventually it was too hard for him even with the sling. We built a ramp for him so that he didn't have to negotiate steps to get outside, and we started carrying him up the stairs to go to bed at night and down the stairs when we woke up in the morning. None of us wanted him to sleep alone downstairs. We all wanted to be together, even when we were sleeping.

He also became unsteady on his feet, prone to losing his balance and falling. So, we got him a harness with a handle on it so that we could literally pick him up off the ground when he had trouble getting up on his own, and could hold on to him if he was walking on uneven ground. While I know there were times he didn't like the harness because it was harder to roll around in the grass with the little handle on his back, there were aspects of the harness that he seemed to enjoy. One of his favorite things was to barrel down the ramp to the backyard, me trotting beside, and then jump off the end of the ramp out into the grass, knowing that I was holding his handle and he could experience the sensation of flying through the air without fear of crashing when he landed. I would always shout, "Wheeeeeee!" as he took flight, and we would have a good laugh.

For years, Gun saw Carol every Wednesday morning at 11 a.m. so that she could put Humpty Dumpty back together again with acupuncture, laser therapy, homeopathic injections in the acupuncture points along his spine, lubrication for his joints, and what I call her "general voodoo." Carol is a very powerful healer, and regardless of the instruments that she chose to effect healing, the reality is that Gunny would often come home from those visits and charge down the hill in the backyard to go on a long walk because he felt so good after seeing her. Wednesday afternoons were often his best time.

And then there was the poop. It had never occurred to me that I would spend the better part of three years of my life cleaning up Gunny's indoor poop until it happened. Poop in the dog bed when we woke up in the morning, poop on the floor, poop on me when I carried him down the stairs and he couldn't hold it, poop that I never even saw hiding on the rug that became camouflaged, smooshed poop, and poop that Gunny let loose in massive quantities while lying on the floor watching TV, never having felt it leave his body. In the latter instance, he sometimes did a double take at the odor and sniffed around as if to say, *"Hmm, something smells funny. Someone must have farted."* It never even occurred to him in the early days that he was the origin of that smell.

Gunny would often wake in the night and freak out because he wanted to go downstairs and get outside in time to poop. He *hated* having accidents in the house, as I think most dogs do. He would go trotting down the hall to the top of the stairs, sometimes pooping as he went. If he wasn't able to make it outside in time and had an accident, his sense of propriety was so strong that he still insisted on going outside in the middle of the night, almost as if to complete a cycle. "One poops outside and even if I already pooped, I should be outside."

We did this for a couple of months but I have to tell you that it was very hard on my back, and worse, it was very hard for me to go back to sleep after carrying a seventy-five-pound dog down the stairs at 3 a.m. and waiting for him to sniff half the backyard before coming back up to bed. I eventually convinced him that it was better to poop on the floor upstairs than to ask me to carry him in the night, and although he didn't like it, he acceded to my request and started doing just that.

We of course took him to see Mark and consulted the entire team, and they invested a lot of time in trying to determine exactly why he was unable to control when he pooped. After pursuing a lot of different avenues, including various medications and tests, they determined that his incontinence was a result of his spinal problems. He just didn't have enough sensation to really feel when it was time to poop, or the ability to control when he did. Mercifully, this condition was also completely painless and posed no risk to his health.

Moreover, I came to actually *rejoice* when he pooped in his bed or in random places at random times. For reasons we never understood, the poops usually were falling out when he felt his best. Carol was the first to notice this; almost infallibly he was the most incontinent when he was ambulating well and feeling well. Perhaps it said something about the tempo of his body and that things were humming along in there. I don't know. I just know that when Gunny was going to the bathroom outside, it was usually not one of his best days. But when he was pooping all over the place, night and day, his tail was usually wagging, his eyes were bright, and he was feeling well.

Why have I described Gunny's pooping problems to you in such gory detail? Because he and I both feel that it is very important for people to realize that just because your dog can't control when he poops, it doesn't mean he doesn't have a good quality of life—assuming that you are cleaning it all up. *Your* quality of life may be affected, but it is not "the end" just because your dog poops himself. If it were, why would your local grocery store have an entire aisle filled with Depends and other adult diapers? It happens to people, too, of course. We don't euthanize them because of it.

People. Gunny had a lot to say about how humans behave—and so do I. How people react to an elderly dog who has trouble getting around, or who accidentally poops in their presence, tells you a lot about them. The judgmental looks that people gave me were sometimes shocking. The head shaking and eye rolling all but said, "How could you keep him around when he can't walk well? What kind of a life is that?" I think some people failed to see that he had a wonderful life, even without great mobility. Physical infirmities didn't mean that Gunny lacked love, imagination, and joy. And I do wonder sometimes if those people who were so quick to judge us actually possessed any real love and joy, even though they walked just fine.

One of my favorite stories in this regard took place in a Waffle House parking lot in North Carolina on one of our road trips. A gentleman in the parking lot just stared at us, watching me hold Gunny's handle while he slowly walked over to the grass to take a pee, and then watched me walk him back to the car. He asked me how old Gunny was (he had just turned fourteen), and inquired about his harness. We explained to him that it was Gunny's "cane" to help him walk. He nodded, and then looked shocked when I hoisted Gun up into my arms and put him into his big Orvis Tempur-Pedic bed in the back of our SUV. The man shook his head and walked away to his car, and I thought, "Oh well, just another person judging us."

Then he turned around and walked back to our car, so I braced myself. He said, "I was just thinking. I hope that I'm that lucky when I'm ninety years old and that someone takes such good care of me."

I had been too quick to judge *him*. Sometimes people amaze you with their callousness, and sometimes they amaze you with their kindness. Gunny made an impression on that man, and I think that it forever impacted his understanding of what love looks like.

Chapter 15

I saw there were these beings full of beautiful light and some had wings. I had seen similar creatures before in Spain. I heard Alexandra mention 'guardian angels' and then one of them spoke to me in a soothing musical voice and I felt something I had never felt before. There was a flood of emotion inside me and I wondered why I hadn't noticed before. Was it just time for me to know of their existence? I just knew I wanted this creature of light, this angel, to stay by my side. I don't always see her but when I call out to her, she comes and lets me know she is there. I've been aware of her presence a lot lately. She is comforting. She sings to me sometimes and tells me not to worry. Laurie is my guardian angel in the flesh, the pink lady my spirit guide. When I look up at the sky I sometimes wonder if I'll just be sucked up by some invisible force but hope my beautiful guardian angel in her pink light will comfort me and guide me to my new home.

Ganimedes

On September 22, 2010, Gunny almost left me for the second time, when he was thirteen years old.

It had been a day like any other — walks, food, snacks, and love. Juan Carlos carried Gun up to bed at about 10 p.m. and sat him down at the top of the stairs. Gun took a few steps towards the bedroom, and then his hind legs gave out and he ended up on his knees, stuck, unable to walk. He looked confused. I picked him up, stood him up on his feet, and thought he was okay. He took another few steps and then literally fell over sideways like a tree. Lights out. Nobody home. Breathing, but completely unconscious.

I freaked out. I was shouting at him, shaking his head in my hands and calling his name, but he was gone. I called Faith, thinking at first that maybe it was a spinal stroke, which could paralyze him, and she told me how to test his reflexes. I couldn't get anything to work. He looked peaceful and was still breathing, but was some place far, far away. I remember saying to Faith, "We are not doing this today. He is not dying today. It is not time. I am not ready."

It had been six years since I had forbidden him to leave me when we were in Switzerland. I had asked him for five more years. Despite all the diseases and surgeries that had befallen him since we left Switzerland, he had given me those five years, plus one more. But it didn't matter — this was all happening too suddenly and I was not ready. I could not accept that he was going to die. Tonight. In my bedroom. With no warning. No.

There was no point in bringing him to a hospital. Whether it was a spinal stroke or a brain stroke, there was nothing to do but wait and see if he woke up and walked. The minutes and hours started to tick by. He wasn't waking up, and he wasn't moving.

I called Alexandra in Los Angeles to tell her what had happened and asked her to try to reach him. I also asked her to draw his aura to see what his energy looked like. She saw some big bad red energy in his brain but didn't know what it was — but I didn't have to be a vet to know that bad energy in his brain was, well, bad. And she saw that his guardian angel, his "pink lady" as he called her, was with him, along with a few more angels. Alexandra was able to talk to him a little and while I don't remember exactly what he told her — we weren't writing things down back then — the gist of it was that he didn't know if he would be able to stay, but that he would try. He just didn't know if he would be able to do it. He said that he felt very far away, like he was floating, and that his guardian angel was with him. That is all we knew.

We stayed up the whole night — Alexandra in Los Angeles and me in Washington, D.C. Juan Carlos and Bacchus were asleep, and I was lying in Gunny's bed, listening to him breathe in the silence of the night. On several occasions, I heard him *not* breathe. While Mark calls this a "long pause" between breaths, we commoners call it *not breathing*. I was positive that he had died in several of those pauses, and then suddenly he would breathe again. Not a big gasp for air, just a quiet breath, then another pause. I called Faith at about 3 a.m. and woke her up because I didn't know what dying looked like and I thought, "This must be it." How could she know if he was dying from her bedroom in another town? But I called and asked her anyway because I was so scared. I put the phone to his ear so that she could tell him how much she loved him and tell him goodbye. She was crying, too.

From 10 p.m. to 7 a.m., I stayed in his bed and held him. I don't think anyone should die alone, but as importantly, I needed to touch him, connect with him, let him *feel* that he was not alone. As the hours passed, I realized that maybe today *was* the day, whether I was ready or not. So I gave him permission to go. He knew that I didn't *want* him to go, but I told him that he didn't have to fight anymore, whispering in his ear, "There is nothing left unsaid or undone between us. You have made me so happy. You are the best thing that ever happened to me, and it is okay. You can go if you need to. I love you."

Nothing changed. He was still "here", but we weren't sure exactly where.

Alexandra sent him Reiki all through the night, but I didn't feel I could do that. I was an energetic mess.

We haven't really talked about Reiki much yet. Reiki is a Japanese word that means "universal healing energy". It is an energy out in the Universe that you can tap into after receiving a series of what are called energy "attunements", which enable you to access the Reiki energy. When you access it, it comes through your head and out of your hands, becoming available to any living being that you are offering it to. That being has to want it, draw it in. You don't force Reiki on anyone—or at least you shouldn't.

I am what is called a Reiki Master Teacher, meaning that I access the energy in a way that promotes healing on a physical, emotional, and spiritual level. The only reason I learned Reiki in the first place was to help Gunny. Even though he had great vets, he needed some extra energy and help on the harder days, and I wanted to help him. I learned to give Reiki long before I opened the pool, and now I use it all the time with the dogs who come to swim. In my experience, most all creatures love Reiki, whether they be human, dog, horse, or chipmunk. It brings them a lot of comfort and pain relief, and most are happy to receive it. I also can send it to anyone long distance, like Alexandra did for Gunny that night. Don't ask me how that is possible or how it works. I don't know. I just know that it does because I have seen the results over and over again.

I had given Gunny so much Reiki over the years that it was a wonder he didn't glow in the dark. He loved it, but I could not give him Reiki that night. All I could do, and what I was led to do instinctively, was pull out negative and ill energy from his body, over and over again, hour after hour. I couldn't see it, but I could feel it. The only time I left Gunny that night was to run back and forth to the bathroom—whatever I was doing was making me sick and I had horrible diarrhea over and over again. But I didn't stop. I felt it was a sign that whatever had made him ill was leaving his body, and even if some of it was accidentally being transferred to me, I didn't care. I just wanted him to live.

The night wore on and as the dawn came, he started to seem a little more present. I called his name, stroked his face, and he opened his eyes briefly. He then rested for a while again. I called Mark at home at about 7 a.m. and he volunteered to come to the hospital on his day off, his foot swollen from a

107

hornet sting, to see Gun. When I spoke to Mark, Gunny wasn't up and walking, but he was alive.

Miraculously, and I do not use that word lightly, by 9 a.m. when we needed to leave for Annapolis, Gunny just stood up. He walked a few steps, stopped to smell Bacchus' weenie as he did every morning, and walked to the top of the stairs to be carried down like nothing had happened. No deficits. No limp. Completely and totally Gunny.

I drove him to Annapolis anyway, and Mark was quite surprised to find a basically normal dog in front of him — well, "Gunny normal" anyway. After checking him from head to toe, Mark ran a few simple blood tests. But whatever had happened to Gunny in the night seemed to have passed. Mark considered it to be a "stroke-like event" and explained to me how some parts of a dog's brain don't have a lot of important stuff to do. So, the stroke must have occurred in one of those parts of his brain, and he had evidently been able to "reroute" its functions to another part. In other words, he had basically rebooted. In fact, he seemed better than before the stroke — much like when your computer is slow and after you reboot it, it seems to process faster.

We will never know exactly what happened that night. But he survived and he was absolutely fine for a very long time after that. I was probably less fine than he. I did not recover from his near-death experience nearly as quickly as he did. As with the illness in Switzerland, it could have gone either way. But the power of our love, along with Alexandra's Reiki and my removal of the harmful energy, saved his life.

Had we done nothing, I do not believe he would have lived. I can't prove it. But that is what I believe.

Chapter 16

An Indian spirit has recently befriended me. He doesn't frighten me. He is nice and talks to me. He said we were both warriors once. We are both looking for a way back to ourselves. He said he would show me how to hunt and fish if he could. That's what he misses most. He was supposed to marry, but she was taken from him. He said we can help each other. He is tired now of wandering, of being stuck here. He says this so Alexandra will know what to do. Alexandra, I hope you can help him. He is eager to move on now. He says he will try to help me when it is my time. I don't want to think about that right now.

Ganimedes

The Native American spirits. Still with us two years after we moved into the house.

Gunny thought it was important to talk about the spirits in this book because he believes that many dogs can see them and they can be terrifying. When we last discussed them, they were alive and well, so to speak, "living" on the land and screwing up the construction and our lives.

111

After Alexandra, Sharon, and I worked on "the spirit problem", I felt that the old man eventually moved on. My view was substantiated by Gunny and Bacchus, who suddenly started going to a corner of the property they previously had avoided at all costs (where we thought the old guy had taken up residence after being kicked out of the house). But Gunny still had periodic panic attacks, and Alexandra continued to see the Native American spirits on the land and in the house. We tried to just live with it since it seemed we didn't have a choice, but they disturbed Gunny greatly.

For both of us, the last straw on the spirit front was one night when I found Gunny down in the basement, under Juan Carlos's desk, *again*. It was almost impossible for Gunny to walk down stairs by himself at that time, but he was so scared that he had gone down to the basement all by himself to hide. When I found him, he was trembling all over. I sat on the floor with him, talked to him, and asked him to please come back upstairs. Nothing doing. I tried getting him to follow me up for a cookie. He refused. That meant this was very serious.

I went back upstairs and called Alexandra, *again*. I was in tears, blubbering, "We just can't live like this anymore. I have to do something." She said, "The spirits are in the house. I will send Reiki from L.A. and ask for protection for the house, and you do Reiki all around the house, as well. Let's see if we can at least get them out of the house."

We hung up, and then she called back a few minutes later. She said, "I was just told why Gunny is afraid of ghosts. It is because he thinks they can take him."

112

My poor sweet boy. No wonder he was terrified. I would have panic attacks, too, if I thought that they could "take me". But why wouldn't he think that? He had seen spirits of sorts when he was close to death in Switzerland, so why wouldn't he associate them with death and leaving this earth? I went back downstairs to talk to him. I told him to listen to me very carefully, and he did.

I said, "Gunny, I know that the ghosts scare you, but they cannot hurt you. They are annoying and rude, but they cannot harm you and they cannot take you. Nobody can take you from me but God, and you will know when it is time. We will talk about it and you will know. Please do not be afraid of them. They are harmless. Please just come back upstairs with me." He stared at me intently for another few minutes, weighing what I had said. And then he got up from under the desk and let me help him back up the stairs.

But that didn't mean that the ghosts were gone. Au contraire. The energy in the pool room sometimes got weird. Dogs who came to swim occasionally got freaked out by things I couldn't see. I could literally see them staring at something in the pool or in the room that was invisible to me. I had a pretty good idea what it was, though. And I certainly wasn't going to embark on the last phase of construction on the house with the ghosts around. So, two years after we moved into the house, I decided to call a shaman to try to solve this problem once and for all.

Where do you find a shaman in the Washington, D.C. area? In my case, I found her through a massage therapist to whom I happened to be telling my ghost stories while she was trying to fix my back. I pretty much ran home after the massage to call Rose, the shaman that the massage therapist had recommended. I explained to Rose that I thought I had a Native American spirit problem and asked if she could help. She said that she could, and made an appointment to come to my house in about two weeks' time.

I did not know anything about shamanism beyond that the word existed and that shamans were healers who, among other things, got rid of bad spirits. I just knew that I was desperate and willing to try almost anything. On the day of our appointment, Rose called and asked me to make a "spirit plate". I said, "I'll be happy to do that, but I have no idea what it is." She told me what to do, so I arranged a plate with nuts and dried fruit, along with some meat and flowers. The purpose of the spirit plate was to make an offering and give energy to the spirits who were coming to assist her. Obviously, they don't physically consume the food, but according to Rose, they take the energy from the food because it requires a lot of their energy to assist in the physical realm.

I had given Rose a thumbnail sketch of what Alexandra and Sharon thought had happened on my land, and she pretty much agreed. She stood on my back porch and pointed to where the Chief was, where the murdering Native American was, and where the young woman who had been murdered was. She also saw two child spirits with the young woman. She confirmed that they had been there for a long time. She said the murderer was trapped in his shame, the young woman was stuck in her rage, and the Chief basically wouldn't leave his daughter.

Rose set up an altar of sorts on the back porch. She had a feather, a drum, some photos, and a long wooden tobacco pipe. We took some loose tobacco and went to the backyard, where we faced east, south, west, and then north. She asked while facing each direction for the "grandmothers and grandfathers" of that direction to be with us and to help the spirits move on, and sprinkled the tobacco around. We also set the spirit plate out in the yard.

We then went back to the porch to sit down, and Bacchus and Gunny joined me. She asked if I wanted the dogs to stay, and I said, "It is really up to them." So she "smudged" all of us for protection since we would all be present.

She told me, "Your only job is to send love and kindness to the spirits. I will do the rest." This would not have been my first instinct; I would have sent anger and frustration if I had not been instructed differently. The minute she started beating her drum, Bacchus high-tailed it inside the house. Gunny, on the other hand, lay at my feet, staring at the backyard, riveted by the whole thing. He didn't budge for the hour that we were out there.

At times, Rose beat the drum really rapidly and at other times more slowly, but like a movie soundtrack, when she was really whacking on the drum I knew the action was getting intense. She was also sweating a lot. The whole process took about forty-five minutes. All of a sudden the drumming stopped and Rose just sat there, exhausted. She looked at me and said, "They're gone."

It's not that I didn't believe her, but since I hadn't seen the ghosts in the first place, how could I know that they were

115

gone? I asked her what had happened, and she said, "I don't remember a lot of it, but it was difficult. I had to ask for my teachers to come and help. The murderer did not realize that he was dead. When my teachers explained to him that he was dead, he left immediately. Next, they helped the young woman to release her rage and move on. Finally, the Chief, his daughter, and the children all transitioned." It was quiet and peaceful in my backyard. There was a "lightness" about the energy that was new. But it was nothing more obvious than that to me.

Next, Rose and I went inside to smudge the interior of the house. I went through the whole house with the smudge stick and Rose beat the drum behind me. We opened up the windows to let all the negative energy out. The same rules seemed to apply to the drum beating for this phase — the faster the drumbeat, the more stuff I knew she was clearing out.

The last place in the house we cleaned was our master bedroom. We went through the room and Rose said that the murderer's energy was "thick like smoke" in there. Lovely. I emphasized, "We really have to be sure it is totally cleaned out, especially because of Gunny." She took another pass through, this time on her knees, and when she came to Gunny's bed, the drum started beating wildly. Most of the negative energy was concentrated right in front of his bed. She didn't know which bed was Bacchus' and which was Gunny's, but all the bad energy was in front of Gunny's bed. My personal theory is that the spirits knew Gunny could see them, so he is the one they hung around. Whether they intended to frighten him or not I do not know, but they did.

116

We cleaned everything up and chatted a bit before she left. I told her about Gunny's Rainbow and why I had built it. "It has been devastating for me to think that I had picked such a great place, only to find that it was full of spirits and bad energy. It is so disappointing to have made such a big mistake. I don't understand how I could have been so wrong."

She told me that I had not been wrong. "It *is* the perfect place for the pool. The land just needed to be healed. There are not many people who would have healed it, and that is why the land chose you. All of the trees and wildlife are so happy that you bought the house and are doing healing work here. It has been sad here for a long time." With the spirits gone, Rose felt that it would be all I had hoped for. She also commented that lots of people in this area have spirit problems, but they don't recognize them as such, so they just end up unhappy, moving, and/or divorced to escape the unhappiness where they live. She felt I was really lucky to have identified the problem so that I could fix it.

We have had no ghost trouble since the day Rose was here. Gunny never had another panic attack. The next phase of construction, while of course not pleasant, was not as traumatic as the prior phases, in the sense that I didn't have lying, thieving, defrauding, incompetent contractors, just regular contractors and regular construction problems. No fires. No public health hazards. No skulls.

Chapter 17

I know I can't make it without the surgery.

Ganimedes

Unfortunately, while Rose was able to heal my land, Gunny still had some problems that clearing the land could not solve. Having survived so much, at almost fourteen years old, the biggest threat to his life was laryngeal paralysis. It is a really terrible degenerative disease, fairly common in old retrievers—especially ones who are weak in the hind end and poop themselves. Essentially, his larynx did not open and close properly, which meant that he was breathing through a very small opening about the size of a straw.

There is no treatment for "lar par", and there is no cure. There is only a "salvage" surgery; they could permanently tie open one side of Gunny's larynx to make a larger opening so that he could breathe. The downside of this surgery was that it would also leave an open path for food and water to go into his lungs because his larynx would never completely close, putting him at risk of aspiration pneumonia for the rest of his life. Without that surgery, he was likely going to suffocate or die of hyperthermia when the heat and humidity hit in summer, unable to cool himself by panting. We had kept the house at 67 degrees for the whole winter, but he had to go outside sometime. And besides that, he was absolutely miserable.

If all went well with the surgery, as it does a large percentage of the time, he would be able to breathe freely again. The biggest risk of the surgery was that he might regurgitate or vomit when he was coming out of anesthesia. If that happened, with his larynx tied open, the stomach acid could come up through his esophagus and go back down into his lungs, causing a horrible, usually fatal, pneumonia. Although there are precautions one can take, there really is no way to control what happens when a dog is waking up from anesthesia.

I had told Mark over the years that we were never going to do tie-back surgery on Gunny. He would get aspiration pneumonia. I just knew it. The least likely thing always happened to him. So, I had secretly hoped that one of his other diseases would kill him before the lar par got any worse. But we worked so hard to treat his liver disease, cut out his thyroid cancer, and manage his orthopedic issues, that he was still very much alive and well, except for the fact that he was becoming unable to breathe.

I talked to Gunny (via Alexandra) about the surgery and asked him what he wanted to do. He knew he could not live without the surgery—he could barely breathe—and he very much wanted to live. It was euthanize him or try the surgery. So, with his blessing, we opted for surgery.

After much research, I decided that the best vet to perform this particular surgery was a surgeon at a hospital in Gaithersburg, Maryland. In other words, my preferred surgeon was not in Annapolis at Mark's hospital, and Mark was not a surgeon so he could not do the surgery himself. This was a real problem because neither Gun nor I wanted to be in a hospital without Mark. But the truth is that the odds were in our favor and I felt this surgeon was the best person for the job.

Since it was the ICU team, not the surgeon, who would be in charge of his post-surgery care, I made an appointment to meet with the head of the ICU, who was a friend of Carol's, to explain Gunny's peculiarities and numerous underlying health issues. Mostly, I tried to help her understand that he was a true "zebra". And that as a warrior spirit, he just never admitted that he was in trouble until it was almost too late. He was just so tough that even in his old age, he never gave more than five minutes' warning that he was going to crash.

I also told her, "We never give up on Gunny. When you have tried everything, and there is only one more thing that you have left to try, however unlikely it might be to work, you try it. We don't give up on Gunny. Ever."

She knew that I was nervous about having Gunny in a hospital without Mark, for whom she had great respect, and she listened patiently and took it all to heart. She accommodated my paranoia by allowing me to hire some of the hospital's off-duty vet techs to sit in the kennel with him after surgery to monitor him for any signs of trouble. Private duty nurses, so to speak. (They were in addition to the techs who were actually *on* duty and whose job it was to monitor him.) Everything was arranged. Every precaution had been taken. We needed to just *do* it.

We picked a surgery date the following week, and there were moments when I worried he would not make it that long. His breathing was just terrible and he was in distress. I almost lost him the night before surgery, thanks to an unusually hot, humid night in April and his horn-dog nature.

For most of his life, Gunny was a humper. A big-time humper. He was an, "I'm the boss of you," authority humper, and he was a horny humper. As a puppy, he made passionate love to his pink blanket, putting on a hump show in front of the television every night. Guests found the twenty-four/seven sex show disturbing, as did we, so we had him neutered at nine months old, expecting that to take care of the problem.

It didn't change a thing. He kept humping. He loved to hump Juan Carlos's leg while Juan Carlos threw the ball to Bacchus. He humped Bacchus any old time. He humped any child who was tall enough to look him in the eye. Once, I caught him pinning a small child to the ground at soccer camp registration while the mom was writing Juan Carlos a check. And poor Chloe, the five-year-old girl who lived next door to us in Switzerland, could not be left alone with Gunny because as soon as she gave him a cookie, he would try to hump her. She would shout, "Arrête! Arrête!" which means "stop" in French, but was always laughing even as her attacker gently pushed her to the ground to hump away.

Why am I telling you this? Because on the night before his surgery, I called Faith—his "girlfriend"—to coordinate plans to meet at the hospital the next day so that she could stay by his side for his surgery. Before we hung up, I put the phone to his ear so she could tell him goodnight. He heard her voice and within moments, he started gathering up his bed in a heap, humping it. His weak hind legs were sliding all over the place, but he wouldn't stop. It had been years since he had tried to hump like that. While it was funny at first, before long he was gasping for air from the exertion of it all, and his larynx was starting to slam shut. Even after I hung up the phone, he wouldn't stop humping that bed. I ultimately had to tranquilize him before he killed himself, all for the pleasure of what might be his very last hump. I sometimes marvel that the stress of living with Gunny didn't kill me long before he died.

We went to the hospital the next morning, ready to get the surgery behind us. I hugged and kissed Gun before they took him to the back, telling him that everything was going to be okay. He headed to the door that would take him to the operating room, looked back over his shoulder at me, and burped. I almost fainted at the thought that he had indigestion before going into surgery. But it was just a burp. He hadn't eaten in over twelve hours and we couldn't wait one more day to operate on him.

The surgery went well. I saw him shortly after his breathing tube was removed, and he was conscious. While no one had ever heard the peculiar sounds he was making when he breathed, they thought he was basically fine. I called throughout the day and night, and the head of the ICU told me she was personally checking on him quite frequently and all was well.

The next morning they asked me to come get him at 2 p.m. to take him home. The ICU chief met me in the lobby to tell me that he looked great, so I could pay the bill and get the car ready—we were going home. What a relief!

I paid the bill, turned on the AC in the car to cool it down for him, and skipped back to the ICU to get him. I took one look at him in the kennel and said to her and the nurses who were unhooking him from the IV, "I don't know why you think he is okay. He is *not* okay. He is *dying!* Right *now*. This *minute*. He's *dying!*" And I was right.

Chapter 18

The worst moment of my life was when I had pneumonia. There was a point when I went down a tunnel and became frightened that I would not be able to find my way back to Laurie or my friends and family and wouldn't have a chance to say goodbye or finish my work here.

Living was still important to me. Feeling like I couldn't breathe was terrifying and I felt paralyzed with fear. It seemed to go on and on and I know I called out to everyone to please hear me to help and you all answered and it was a huge relief to finally see white light trickling into my head and I could see all of your faces and knew you were all willing me to survive, to find my way home.

It was horrible, but it showed me what the human spirit is about especially when they join forces. I'm still working on why these particular people care so much but know that is what makes them unique. Even at my lowest moment, I knew if we all tried I would have more time.

Ganimedes

My warning stopped the vet in her tracks. She calmly replied, "Well, he does look different than he did a few minutes ago." But they didn't seem too alarmed. They took his temperature and his pulse, which were normal. The vet listened to his chest and seemed a little unsure. I called Alexandra in L.A. to see if she could talk to him because it was clear to me he was losing consciousness and nobody had a clue what was happening—they had not even come to the medical conclusion that something was wrong. But I knew he was dying, and I needed Gunny to tell us what he could before it was too late.

Alexandra was able to reach him, but just barely. All he said was, *"I'm dizzy and I can't see. I want Mark."* I relayed this to the vet, and they whisked him away to do a chest x-ray. Meanwhile, I called Mark, who agreed to come from over an hour away simply because Gunny asked him to.

The x-ray revealed that Gunny had aspiration pneumonia, in both lungs, likely because he had regurgitated stomach acid into his lungs at some point after surgery. They immediately put him in a Plexiglas oxygen box that was just barely big enough to hold him and cranked up the oxygen. Even that fancy box could not make enough oxygen for him to breathe, so they had to put in extra oxygen hoses to get enough oxygen in the box. The oxygen gauge in Gunny's box hovered between 70 and 75 percent supplemental oxygen, and he needed every bit of it because his lungs were so full of pneumonia. He could breathe in the box, but with great difficulty. He lay there, stretching his neck as high as it would go, trying to get a clear path from his nose to his lungs.

In the twenty-four hours after his surgery, he had sat under everyone's watchful eye, including the off-duty techs' gaze, and almost suffocated to death right in front of them *and no one noticed*. The problem, in part, was his "zebra" nature. At no point did he raise a fuss or complain at all. But obviously, if they had monitored his oxygen levels more frequently, they would have known he was in trouble. Had I not been there at 2 p.m., he probably would have died. For that matter, had they discharged him earlier in the day, we would have been home when he went into a respiratory crisis and I would not have been able to save him. The fates had intervened, but only up to a point. He was in critical condition.

Mark and Faith both came to the hospital that night to see him. They sat with Juan Carlos and me in front of his oxygen box, just talking to him, letting him know that they were there for him. The doctors started him on three different IV antibiotics, with Mark's blessing, and told us to just wait and see if the antibiotics worked. There wasn't much else to do. Statistically, he was unlikely to survive because the pneumonia was so severe.

When everyone left, I sat outside his oxygen box and I asked him directly what he wanted to do.

"Do you want to stay, or are you ready to go? It's okay to go," I told him. "I know you are tired and very sick. I'm so sorry that this happened to you. I'm so, so sorry." It was pretty much the same conversation we had had after his stroke, except this time he was conscious.

He looked back at me with razor-sharp focus, his eyes glistening, and said, *"You get me out of this damned box and get me the hell home."* His answer was very clear to me. He was not ready to die.

Alexandra spoke to him, too. He was a little more philosophical with her: *"The heart is willing. Let's see what the body can do."*

After a couple of days, it was pretty clear that the antibiotics were not working, notwithstanding his heart's willingness. He was not eating, and he was very sick. He could not leave the box for any reason, not even to go to the bathroom. His life depended on that 75 percent oxygen environment. And as he himself told you, he was terrified because it was so hard to breathe. On day three of this ordeal, I met with one of the vets, whom I dubbed Dr. Fancy Pants because, although she was very smart, her know-it-all manner rubbed me the wrong way. She told me that Gunny's blood oxygen levels were worse and that this was a very dire situation. She was certainly right about that. The oxygen level in his arterial blood, which carried oxygen to his brain and organs, should have been 100 percent with him on supplemental oxygen. It was only 50 percent. It is hard to conceive of how he was even alive at that oxygen level, since as a practical matter, it is not a lot different from being dead.

The way she delivered this information, as opposed to the news itself, just annoyed the shit out of me. All the vets at this hospital, other than the ICU chief, talked to me like I was a person who didn't understand Gunny's condition or was an irrational emotional basket case. I understood perfectly well. I was neither in denial nor irrational. No one needed to "prepare" me for the possibility that he would die.

I understood what the expected outcome was, but what I *also* knew, and what they *didn't*, was what Gunny and Team Gunny were capable of in a life or death situation. He wanted to go home, and however unlikely, it was still *possible* that he would, because Team Gunny was working overtime.

After my conversation with Dr. Fancy Pants, I walked back to the ICU to visit him, but when I got about halfway there, I heard them call a "Code Blue". People started running, just like they do on TV, and one vet yelled to me, "It's you!" There were fifteen dogs in that ICU, but I had already known it was him. When I walked into the ICU they had him on the stainless steel table in the middle of the room. He had gone into a respiratory crisis, but he was starting to stabilize. I stood in front of him and offered him Reiki. It was the only thing I could do. And the only thing that was really going to help at that moment.

Dr. Fancy Pants came to talk to me about what to do next. Basically, she gave me the choice to euthanize him or, as a long shot, to switch him to a stronger antibiotic, imipenem, which is reserved for antibiotic-resistant infections (as his apparently was) and which cost $800 a day. I really couldn't focus on anything other than sending Gunny Reiki in that moment, which took both my hands and a focused mind. So, in the best tone of voice I could muster, I said, "Please get my cell phone out of my purse and hand it to me." I grabbed it, scrolled down to Mark's name, hit *Call* and handed her the phone. "When the phone rings, Mark is going to answer. Please explain everything to him and then pass me the phone when you are through."

This was disrespectful and impolite, but I really did not care about etiquette at that moment. I just needed Mark to understand what was happening and to tell me what to do. She didn't understand Gunny and she didn't understand me. Her judgment was based on textbooks, and our experience suggested that whatever was going to happen next was not going to be found in a textbook. The rules and statistics rarely applied to us.

Mark thought we should try the imipenem. Juan Carlos also felt very strongly that we should try it. He just had a good feeling about the antibiotic and thought that it would work and that Gunny would be okay. Gun had given me seven years since Switzerland, and I did not want him to suffer anymore. I was so overwhelmed at the thought of losing him that I couldn't think straight. I deferred to the guys, and we started the imipenem.

Gunny's body was exhausted from the pneumonia and all that had preceded it. Even after being on the imipenem for two days, he had another breathing crisis. This time, his arterial oxygen level had plummeted to 41.5 percent, forcing a conversation about whether we wanted to put him on a ventilator if he became unable to breathe on his own again, or whether we wanted to euthanize him. The ICU chief said, "It is close to 100 percent certain that he will never come off the ventilator if you put him on it, and if he were my dog, I would not put him through it." But she also said, "I know you, and all that you have been through, and I am afraid that if you don't try it, you will regret it for the rest of your life."

They suspected that he not only had pneumonia, but also some other sort of respiratory complication and that he was not going to get better. (This sounded a lot like when the vets in Switzerland told me, "We think his bone marrow is dead so even if you get the platelets, we don't think he can live.") The truth is, nobody, not even Mark, knew what exactly was wrong or what was going to happen. But the situation was clearly pretty bad.

I tracked down Gunny's vet team that night to try to reach consensus about whether, if another crisis came, we should try the ventilator, knowing it was a long shot. Peter knew one dog who had come off a ventilator. One was better than none. Everyone, including Juan Carlos, voted, "Yes." I was reluctant because I thought the kindest thing to do might be to just let him go if he had another crisis. And then I remembered my own words before the surgery: "If there is only one thing left to try, no matter how unlikely it is to work, we try it. We never give up on Gunny." It felt as though I had put a message in a time capsule and sent it to myself in the future. We were unanimous in deciding to try the ventilator if it became necessary, so at midnight the hospital staff got busy setting it up so that it would be ready if the time came.

I spent the night in the back of my SUV in the hospital parking lot that night. I had gone to visit Gun at 4 p.m. and never left. I knew that he could die at any moment, and I could not bear the thought of him dying without me. I spent the night in the car, cell phone in hand, ready to run into the hospital to be with him if he was dying. I didn't sleep much, of course, and I called from the car to the ICU to get updates throughout the night from the ICU chief, who normally left work by 10 p.m. but had stayed most of the night out of concern for Gunny. We had a long chat about how Gunny had ended up in this disastrous position, and she had the time to talk because although everyone remained on high alert, he was holding steady in the night. By 6 a.m., they felt that he had stabilized, so I drove home to catch a nap before visiting hours started again at 10:30 a.m. I, of course, was relieved, but part of me was also disbelieving that he would be okay given how things had unfolded up to this point.

Team Gunny pulled out all the stops to get us through the crisis. Everyone was praying for him and sending him love, and I conveyed to him all the dozens of email messages that Team Gunny was sending his way:

"Ganimedes, we are all with you!"

"Gunny, you can do this, you are a tough ole boy!"

"Be strong beloved Gunny. We love you and need you. Our love is complete and unconditional."

"Fight, Gunny, fight."

And our favorite group chant, "Go, Gunny, go!"

Eventually, the imipenem worked and he started to feel better. Much like the platelet shipment to Switzerland, the ventilator was at the ready but never needed. But it was still a long road to recovery. His veterinary team stood by him throughout. Carol came to give him acupuncture to help with his emotional state as well as his pneumonia. Faith came to massage and laser him because he was getting so sore from not moving. Mark came to visit him because he knew that it made Gunny feel better to see him. Alexandra sent him Reiki more or less ten hours a day until she was exhausted. Not one of them let me pay them for their time.

I stayed with Gun as much as the hospital permitted, which was usually four to five hours a day. He was pretty weak and there was really nothing to do, but as always, we felt better just being together. I sometimes curled up in his bed with him, napping and holding his paw. Other times, I talked to him for hours, telling him what was going on in the world and at the pool so that he didn't miss out on too much while he was in the hospital. We talked about starting construction at the house, the recent royal wedding of William and Kate, and the fact that Juan Carlos was going to be really mad if Gun even thought about eating all the grass he had just planted in the front yard. Rolling in it would have to do.

Gunny managed to communicate with me now and then even when I wasn't at the hospital. One night, I woke in the middle of the night with a very vivid picture in my head. I saw a tall and handsome man with a big beard, a middle-aged woman, and a young girl with long hair, all standing together. It was clear from their clothes that they lived in another time long ago, but I didn't recognize it as a particular historical period (my world history knowledge is just not that good). I knew that Gunny had sent me the mental image, and for some reason, I felt that he was the tall man and I was the young girl in another lifetime. I don't know why I thought that, but I was certain of it.

The next communication from his hospital bed was far more comical. About two days before he was released, when he was just starting to eat again, he sent me a very clear message while I was in the shower. *"I want a McDonald's hamburger and fries."* I cracked up laughing, and answered back that it would have to wait until he was out of the hospital. His stomach wasn't up to Mickey D's quite yet.

The last few days he was hospitalized were free of crisis or conflict. While I felt that they had made mistakes that could have cost Gunny his life, I also had appreciated over the course of his hospitalization how hard most of the staff was working to help him heal and keep him as comfortable as possible, given his condition. For example, they kept him out in the middle of the room when they could, rather than in the kennel, so that he had company and so that they could easily keep an eye on him. He lay on a stack of cushions and pillows two feet tall that was the envy of the other dogs. And the last couple of days, when he was out of the oxygen box and only on nasal oxygen, I begged them to let him get some sunshine after so many days indoors. They hooked up about thirty feet of oxygen tubing from his kennel and carried him outside like a king, on his big pillowed bed, so that he could enjoy some fresh air while he was still on supplemental oxygen.

He came home on May 6, 2011, twelve days after he checked in for a one-night surgical stay. He walked out of the hospital on his own power, with about a half dozen of the hospital staff clapping and cheering for him as he left. The warrior was not carried out on his shield after all. He had won another battle. He had survived against all odds.

Chapter 19

Bacchus wouldn't have survived me leaving then. We have grown so close. I have so much to tell him still so he can be happy when I'm gone. He thinks there is too much responsibility of being the dog in charge, that he wouldn't be able to do all that is required of him, but he has been doing just that for a long time now, he just doesn't realize it. What I'm trying to get across to him is that he is capable and he already does what he needs to do because in reality nothing is required of him but to be Bacchus. He has an innocent nature, unlike me. I want him to know we are more, much more than just dogs. We have a soul like all living creatures. This is one of the reasons I continue on.

When Laurie started talking about Bacchus being sick, I was surprised. He's always been a fine specimen of a dog. There have been moments when my dog self was jealous that Bacchus can still run and jump and swim with ease, and bumps in the road don't seem to bother him the way they do me. But when I think about it, I knew something wasn't quite right. I wouldn't wish being sick on anyone. I thought he would always be fine and now I realize that is not necessarily true.

I have been very concerned about Bacchus. I realize our life can be taken from us at any moment without warning. I don't want my brother to suffer the way I have. He is my little brother and a faithful companion and friend. I know he has depended on my guidance through the years, but he still has a mind of his own. I may have been the one he always looked up to but he has been my grounding force. Now he knows it's not fun on the other side of those doors at the vet's office and it's my turn to wait and wonder. I'm sorry he got sick.

Ganimedes

Gunny's battle with pneumonia changed everything. He was not the same. I was not the same. Juan Carlos and Bacchus were not the same. Even the house was not the same—the workmen had started excavating for our next phase of construction while he was in the hospital, so there was noise and construction chaos yet again.

Gunny was weak and required around-the-clock care, including antibiotic injections that I gave him three times a day for six weeks. I had not worked, eaten, or slept much for the two weeks that he was in the hospital. Now that he was home, I had a new set of duties. I cooked for him, massaged him, gave him Reiki, and devoted myself to him with my whole being. This was our new normal. But none of it felt like a burden. I was just so happy to have him back home! Little by little, he got his strength back. After being cooped up inside the hospital for so long, it was time to revel in a really beautiful Washington spring.

When I wasn't swimming dogs, Gun and I sat in the front yard for hours a day watching people go by, enjoying the sunshine, and reading *A Dog's Purpose*. I read to him in full read-aloud voice—with exclamations and pauses for effect and different voices for different characters. Gun would lie in the sun alternating between smiling, listening, yawning, and napping while I read to him for hours. He enjoyed the whole experience of being outdoors, breathing freely again, and listening to the sound of my voice.

In the book, which is fiction, a dog recounts his various lifetimes, some good, some bad. The book traces the dog's love for a little boy he had grown up with in one of his early dog lives, to a time decades later when as a different dog, he is reunited with the boy, who is now an old man. Seemed perfect for us! I wondered if perhaps we had a similar history—maybe Gunny had been my dog in another life and that is why our connection was so strong. It was a far more plausible scenario than believing we were the man and girl he had shown me the mental picture of when he was hospitalized. The idea that he had been my dog before seems funny now, but at that point, I had only an inkling of what our connection truly was.

In the immediate aftermath of the pneumonia, there is no doubt that Gunny got even more attention than usual, and that Bacchus did not get his fair share. Bacchus had a wonderful life by any standard and we loved him so very much, but his brother's constant health challenges demanded a lot from us. To his credit, Bacchus never acted out to get attention. He just did his part to help support Gunny and made our lives easy by being a very good boy. I did not love Bacchus less, but I loved him differently. And he knew it.

> *I don't even mind anymore that [Gunny] is Laurie's favorite. He explained to me how they have known each other before and have had things to work out together. I really don't understand that but I will accept it because I love him and I know he wants the best for me and he cares. I know in my heart that Laurie loves me, too. Gunny says, 'Love is love, but it shows itself in different ways.' He said he might leave soon and I don't want him to. I'm scared and don't want him to talk about it anymore. I love him.*

When I first read that Bacchus thought Gunny was my favorite, I was truly horrified. I felt like a terrible mother who had neglected one of her children. And truthfully, one of my greatest fears for many years had been that Bacchus would get sick and that I would be too busy taking care of Gunny to notice. As it turned out, despite all that focus on Gunny, thank God, I didn't miss it when Bacchus gave me the sign.

Shortly after Gunny came home, Bacchus just didn't seem himself. There were so many perfectly good explanations for that, between the trauma of Gunny being gone and the construction at the house, not to mention my having gone a little crazy through it all. But in addition to an amorphous feeling that he was a little "off", there were a couple of things that had my attention. In particular, we found that Bacchus had pooped in the basement several times, which was just weird. The back door, which they normally used to go outside, was now blocked off due to the excavation so the boys had to go out the front door to go to the bathroom. But still.

I hadn't been able to shake a sense of impending doom ever since Bacchus had told Alexandra, while Gun was hospitalized with pneumonia, that he didn't want to live without Gunny. He said that he wanted "*to go to the Big Dream with Gunny.*" Gunny was still present and accounted for, but Bacchus had gotten himself in quite a state thinking about the possibility that Gunny might not come home from the hospital.

So I brought Bacchus to see Mark on June 24—about six weeks after Gun came home from the hospital. Mark was smarter than anyone I knew, and had known me long enough to know that if I told him there was something wrong with my dog, there probably was. If anyone was going to figure it out, or have the credibility to tell me I was wrong, it was Mark.

I told him, "I just have a bad feeling. I want you to check every bit of him from nose to tail—abdominal ultrasound, chest x-rays, blood work."

Mark did as I asked, and the preliminary findings were . . . that I was crazy. (My words, not his.) Everything was perfect. The only thing he found, on ultrasound, was a very tiny irregularity in Bacchus' prostate that was only one centimeter big. Although it was likely nothing more than a benign growth, he stuck a needle in it to take some cells for analysis, just in case.

The pathology report was definitive: Bacchus had prostate cancer. For those of you who are breathing a relative sigh of relief thinking, "Well, if you have to have cancer, that's a good one to have," you are wrong. In dogs, it is horribly metastatic, grows quickly, and is almost impossible to treat effectively. Surgery is painful and leaves them incontinent, and never gets all the cancer anyway. Many dogs die within a few months of a prostate cancer diagnosis because they are no longer able to pee or poop due to blockage from the tumor; some are euthanized on the day they are diagnosed because it was the inability to pee in the first place that brought them to the doctor. It was very, very bad news.

I talked to our veterinary team, and everyone seemed to think that because we caught the cancer so incredibly early, stereotactic radiation, which you may know as CyberKnife, was our best and only shot. Stereotactic radiation is a very precise and powerful type of radiation that was originally invented to irradiate inoperable brain tumors in people. Over time, they have found more uses for it in other types of cancer that are hard to get to, like prostate cancer. It was incredibly rare to find a prostate tumor at such an early stage, so we needed to pull out all the stops to give Bacchus the best possible chance at survival.

At the time, there were only three stereotactic radiation machines for veterinary use in the United States. None of them were in the Washington, D.C., area. When I called the vets who ran the programs at each of the three hospitals to ask about their experience with prostate cancer, the math was simple: only seven dogs in the entire country had ever been treated with stereotactic radiation for prostate cancer.

"Of the seven dogs that had received the treatment," I asked, "how many of those dogs are still alive?"

The answer was, "Zero." And most had only lived a few months.

But Bacchus' tumor was a lot smaller than the other dogs' had been.

Of the three veterinarians using stereotactic radiation machines, I chose Dr. Nick at the University of Florida in Gainesville. For tangible and intangible reasons, I thought he was the best chance Bacchus had. He is wickedly smart, almost as stubborn and opinionated as me, and 100 percent committed to whatever he is doing. When I told Nick that I believed we could *cure* Bacchus, he did not act like I was in denial or stupid. He told me that it was unlikely—but he didn't tell me it was not possible. This made him an optimist compared to the others. Regardless of what he thought about the chances, he knew I was not trying to buy Bacchus some time. I was trying with all my might to *cure* him. After all, Bacchus presented the best chance anyone had yet seen to cure prostate cancer in a dog.

My request of Nick was simple. "I am going to throw a Hail Mary pass, and I need you to catch it." For a Brit, turns out Nick is a hell of a wide receiver.

Chapter 20

I'm happy that Gunny cares so much about me. I sometimes didn't know. I really don't like feeling bad but am glad that Laurie is helping. I don't understand what they are doing to me. I get scared sometimes and want my dad with me more. I wish Juan Carlos could be with me all the time. When he isn't here I worry.

I heard Laurie talking about what is happening to me so I closed my eyes and hoped we could go home soon. I didn't like Florida and worried about Gunny and Laurie and me. I don't want to ever go back there even though everyone was nice. I was scared and lonely and confused. I am trying. I like to swim but sometimes I feel tired. Why is that? I feel sick sometimes. It isn't a good feeling. I want to be told what to do and that this will go away.

Bacchus

Gunny turned fourteen about a week after we learned Bacchus had cancer. We had a big birthday party for him on July 4th with his human and dog friends, and we had "Good Luck Bacchus" cake along with Gun's birthday cake. Gunny got some great presents. Peter and Faith brought the boys McDonald's cheeseburgers, their favorite. His Aunt Ana and Uncle Jack got him a fifty-dollar gift certificate to McDonald's — are you detecting a theme? And our friends Bob and Sherri had a star named after him, and gave us the coordinates so that we could find it in the sky. Everyone at the birthday party knew we were hoping to go to Florida within a few days, and Bacchus had the benefit of everyone wishing him well and telling him that he would be fine. I'm sure he was a little perplexed as he didn't really feel bad at this point, but I can guarantee that he was happy basking in all the love directed his way, too. All in all, July 4, 2011 was a lovely day.

Nick called me the next morning to tell me that if we could be in Gainesville the following day at 11 a.m., we could start treatment before he left on a trip. I actually took that call while I was in the pool with one of my dog clients. I booted the dog out of the pool, walked into the house dripping wet and told Juan Carlos, who was in a meeting with a contractor, to finish the meeting and start packing.

"Why?" he said.

"Because we're leaving for Florida in an hour," was my reply.

One of the difficult decisions we had to make was whether to take Gunny with us to Florida. Given the condition of his spine, joints, and already tense muscles, riding in a car for two straight days had the potential to be catastrophic for him. And I was terrified to take him away from his weekly visits with Carol and the rest of his veterinary team. However, that had to be weighed against several factors. I had to be the one to stay with Bacchus in Florida because Juan Carlos was in the middle of summer soccer camp. In addition, it was hard to imagine Gunny being okay without me for a couple of weeks. He was very emotionally and physically dependent on me and would not have done well separated from me for so long. Third, I really believed that Bacchus' emotional well-being hinged on having his brother with him. Gunny was his leader and his best friend, and I thought Bacchus would come apart without Gunny by his side.

When we got to Florida, Bacchus had a full-body CT scan to see if they saw any metastasis in his lymph nodes or elsewhere. We had nothing but good news! No cancer anywhere else, and a tiny but clear tumor to shoot at. We were ready to go kill his cancer cells with Nick's fancy machine.

In the midst of Bacchus' cancer treatment, Gunny started falling apart. I don't know what happened and neither did Gunny. The heat was certainly insufferable and I know it was hard for him to make the trip to the hospital almost every day and wait around for news about Bacchus. I lugged his bed into the hospital lobby every day so he would be more comfortable, and got him physical therapy treatments to try to keep him going. The wheels started coming off the truck anyway. Five days after we arrived, on a Saturday night, I thought he was going to die right there in our hotel room. He looked like he was in terrible pain, but more than that, he looked sick. Not just orthopedically messed up, but sick. I found blood on the sheets where he was sleeping, both in his saliva and in his urine. He was very lethargic, and when I asked Alexandra to talk to him, he said, *"I don't know if I am going to be able to make it home."* Let's just say I didn't take it

145

well. I was completely alone, with the responsibility of saving not one, but two dogs on my shoulders.

I told Gunny to just forget about dying in Florida. It wasn't going to happen. This wasn't one of those touchy-feely, heart-to-heart talks. I just flat told him he couldn't do it. Not open for discussion. We would see Uncle Mark and figure out what was happening when we got back to Washington, but we *had to get home*. I was all but carrying Gunny outside to the bathroom because he was so weak, and Bacchus was distraught about all the anesthesia and medical treatments he was having. Now he was also worrying that his brother was going to die. I remember lying down on the couch in the hotel room that weekend, and Bacchus climbing up on the sofa to lie lengthwise on top of me, his head on my chest and his body stretched out all the way to my feet. He went to sleep like that, with me gently stroking his back. I'm not sure who was hugging whom that afternoon.

There was no easy explanation for why Gun had fallen apart. They did various tests at the university hospital on Monday and found nothing. Amazingly, I found a holistic vet in Gainesville who agreed to come to the hotel to see if she could help Gunny. I can't explain what she did, but I can tell you that when she arrived, Gunny wouldn't get up to greet her and more or less lay on his side for most of the three hours she was there working on him. By the time she left, he stood up on his own and stole a shoe to play with.

With her help, Gunny improved every day and was feeling more like himself. It later became clear that Gunny's spleen had probably bled while we were in Florida, and whatever she did appeared to have helped his body repair the damage and recover.

Meanwhile, Bacchus had his third and final radiation treatment on July 15th, my birthday, and was doing great. It looked like we were all going to make it out of Florida alive.

Chapter 21

I don't know exactly when I realized who I was. I didn't really think about it. As time went on, I knew I had my own thoughts and desires, but wasn't aware of my limitations until I was about two and a half. I remember looking around me one day. I'm not sure where we were, out for a walk somewhere, when I thought, 'Wait a minute. That woman walking down the street used to be someone I knew or thought I knew.' She was wearing a hat and a dress. Everything looked familiar but different. I was confused and wondered how I had gotten there. I remember looking in a puddle of water and seeing a dog's face look back at me and remember saying to myself, 'That's not me. I'm a man.' At least I thought I was a man. It was a shock because the realization just came upon me so abruptly.

Then I thought, 'Maybe this is a dream.' But it turned out it wasn't. It was like I had amnesia, but now I was beginning to remember little things. I felt trapped at first. I don't think I came to terms with it for a long time. My instincts were not always my own but [those] of a dog. It was like going in and out of consciousness. I eventually settled into my body and my life. Somehow I knew not to fight it. I would take one day at a time and see what happened. How many times have I said to myself if [I] just go along with what is happening then this duality will be over and I will be my true self again.

My life with Laurie and Juan Carlos has been very interesting, full of ups and downs, travel, fun, sorrow, beauty, stress, and love. I watched them for many years waiting to see what would happen. When would they see that I was more than their beloved furry friend?

Ganimedes

When we returned home from Florida in July, Gunny began an intense dictation period with Alexandra. He was not always feeling well during this time, but he was determined to write. She would send me pages as he dictated them, and reading them was like watching a flower bloom, a new petal opening up every day. I don't know if Gun understood what was happening any more than we did, but it seemed that the more he talked and opened himself up, the more he changed and grew. He started to remember other lifetimes he had lived as a man, not a dog. A lot of what he said was simply hard to believe, but he spoke so clearly that it was equally hard to disbelieve.

Unfortunately, at the end of August—just a month or so after returning from Florida—we discovered that Gunny's spleen had gone bad. He was periodically bleeding internally, which made him very weak and sick, and at some point in the not-too-distant future, his spleen was probably going to explode. Not the medical term, obviously, but *de facto* what was going to happen. I left the decision about whether to have spleen surgery up to him. And this time I really meant it. He kept expecting me to make the decision for him, as I always had, and I refused. I was heartsick at the thought of another surgery, and equally heartsick at the thought of losing him. For his whole life, I had felt that I knew what was best for him, but this time, I honestly didn't. I could not choose for him one more time; he was going to have to figure out what he really wanted. It was the first time that he was totally responsible for a medical decision, and he didn't like it one bit.

Alexandra spoke to him over and over again about what he wanted to do, and each time she did, he had a different answer about what he wanted. What it boiled down to was this—he was pissed that something else had gone wrong. He did not want to have surgery again, but he also was not quite ready to die. Without surgery, he was definitely going to die, either from an exploding spleen or because I would have to euthanize him to avoid his spleen rupturing and his bleeding to death.

> *I have been preparing myself to go. I have made peace with my life this time around. I have made peace with my body as well. I don't feel well a lot of the time. I don't feel like fighting for my life anymore. I wouldn't*

151

mind staying a little longer but I don't want to stay much longer.

This is all so exhausting for Laurie and I want her to STOP. Just stop trying to make it all right. I am fine on my own. Of course I want to feel good and don't want to be sick, but I am sick. I am ready to leave when it's my time. Laurie you can't decide that for me. No. I don't want the surgery.

I have finished what I have wanted to accomplish as much as I can in this body. I know I will be able to accomplish more on the other side. It will not be the end. I finally realized I'm not immortal. My body isn't anyway. I do believe in life after death.

[You ask me] if I had the surgery and could stay a few months longer would I want that? NO! I don't want the surgery. I want to be left alone. Do I want to write? Yes, of course.

So he kept writing, and within a couple of days, his view about surgery softened. *"If I'm still alive in a week, I'll have the surgery."*

The next seven days were like living in Disneyland for Gunny and Bacchus, who seemed no worse for the wear after his radiation treatments and was feeling pretty good. We went away for a few days to the shore, which always made them happy and was a change of pace. We took them to dinner at Mia's Pizzeria, where we sat outside on the patio listening to a jazz trio while they happily munched pizza crust and enjoyed the music. We went to special places for short walks. And we loved each other totally, completely, and madly. For all we knew, these were our last days together as a family.

I scheduled his surgery a week out, praying he would make it. And I rallied Team Gunny. This time, in addition to their usual dedication, they also involved medicine men and monks. Our friend who was in Bali at the time asked Ketut, the famous medicine man from *Eat, Pray, Love* to send an encouraging message to Gunny and say a prayer for him. Not to be outdone, a friend who lives in Bhutan had five Bhutanese and Tibetan monks who were visiting his home pray for him and hold up "Go, Gunny, Go" signs, which he photographed for me to show Gunny. Literally, people all over the world were cheering him on and rallying others to the cause, just as they had done so many times before.

In October, Gun had what we all knew was going to be his last surgery, this time in Annapolis, where Mark could watch over him. Surgery went off without a hitch, but he was very slow to wake up. Although he was rouseable, he was essentially unconscious for the entire day after the surgery. Faith figured he was off on an adventure and wasn't too worried. I was really scared he wasn't coming back. As usual, thank goodness, Faith was right.

Chapter 22

As you know, after yet another surgery, I'm still here! Yes I am glad I had the surgery otherwise I would be begging for release. Part of me wanted to go, part wanted to stay. Life is precious after all and unless I am in unbearable pain or distress I will try to ride it out.

I've been busy gathering my friends, old and new, on the other side. When I was unconscious during surgery, the people in white came back. I first saw the man in white I spoke of before, who was impressed with my aptitude for being in more than one place at once and was happy with my progress. My experience with him made me want to do more while I'm still here but I'm not sure what that is. I saw the most beautiful swirling colors and planets and clouds and far away stars and suns as we went through space at an accelerated speed. I asked for my guardian angel to accompany me since I feel comfortable around her, trust her, and knew I wouldn't be frightened if she was there. I was excited to tell you [Alexandra] and Laurie about this adventure.

That's why I slept so long after the surgery. They took me flying around and showed me many things. They showed me my heritage as a human. We went way back in time. I was shown many people who made an impact on my many lives. The first captain when I was a sailor was there. He is a guide for me. I asked him why he was there. He said that we had a connection and it's part of his job right now, to help others who have crossed his path. His name is John. He's earning his wings. I don't know if that's literal but that's what he told me. I saw a woman who said that she had been my mother from another life. I really didn't recognize her. She said not to worry. I didn't owe her anything but she said she wanted me to experience as much love as possible, then she left. My heart is so open. I still don't know what this all means.

I still have some fear about leaving my body but she and John, the Indian spirit, Max and Winston and my guardian angel said they will be there. I am a lucky man. I didn't want the feeling to end. I hated the way it felt to be back in my body after feeling so free, but I was so grateful and happy to be with my family again. I am thankful I have been able to be here for Bacchus, to make sure he recovers. I think he will try harder and desire it more if I am here. That was one of the reasons I wanted to stay. I didn't think Laurie was quite ready either. I felt Juan Carlos

would be greatly saddened. When I go, I want you to
all be happy for me because my adventure is all new
this time around and I won't be alone. I needed to tell
all of you that. I love you all so much.

Ganimedes

Gunny recovered from his spleen surgery very quickly, and the next few months were some of the best days that we all had together in the last year of his life. Bacchus was feeling great. Gunny was feeling great. The construction was winding to a close, and everything seemed right with the world. Gunny felt well enough for the boys to go on walks together again, and they were closer than ever. There was no particular event that made this time good. It was more the relative, albeit brief, respite from the constant worry we had lived with since April when Gunny almost died. For now, neither of them seemed at risk of dying in the immediate future, and we had a few months of normalcy.

Normalcy meant we still had the day-to-day struggles of helping Gunny, but they were manageable. For example, he had to be fed every four hours around-the-clock, day and night, to try to control his seemingly uncontrollable acid reflux. While for most dogs reflux would be unpleasant, for Gunny, it was life threatening because of the tie-back surgery. So, I never slept more than three hours or so at a time.

Although Gunny was feeling much better without his spleen, orthopedically, he was now at a point where he often needed help to get up off the floor and was at a constant risk of falling. He did not want me to leave the house, pretty much ever. But if I did, he wanted to know that I would return within "*three hours to come say hello or give [him] a snack. I like being told where you are going and when you will be coming back. Now being old and some of my senses impaired I need more of you, as you know. Time is not always a straight line for me anymore.*" So I would tell him where I was going and how long it would be before I returned. But mostly, I just never left him.

Bacchus captured it all succinctly.

I know it's hard for Laurie that Gunny can't get around easily anymore. Sometimes I wish we were all young again. I don't feel as young anymore. I don't know what will happen tomorrow or after that. I know that Laurie has hardships and worries. I wish she didn't have worries. She takes good care of me and I am glad she loves me. I want her to be happy.

Honestly, I was so happy to have everyone relatively well and on an even keel that I felt really lucky, even though I was exhausted. Gunny was now fourteen-and-a-half years old and Bacchus was ten. What we all really wanted was one last trip to Spain together. But when we thought it over, it just didn't make sense. Gunny was in no shape to be traveling across the Atlantic Ocean in a cargo hold. But we all needed to get out of Bethesda, Maryland, for a while. We decided that the warm weather of Florida would have to do.

Chapter 23

I have moments when I don't understand how I got here and how or why all these things are happening. And then I look down at the shoreline, and I see millions and millions of shells — all sizes and shapes but mostly in the shape of a scallop shell. And I know that this is my path and I am where I am supposed to be in this moment. I just need to find a yellow arrow.

Laurie, Sanibel Island

January 2012

I have walked the Camino de Santiago every few years because I have found that it keeps me grounded. Walking with other pilgrims always reminds me that I am no different from anyone else — we all have our struggles, both big and small. And I know that every time I walk, I will learn something. Usually a lesson I didn't even know that I needed to learn. So, I have sought out the Camino periodically for what it can teach me if I'm paying attention, or to work out a problem or clear my head.

On one trip, for example, we dedicated our walk to Gunny, carrying a stone to the Iron Cross, where pilgrims leave a rock in order to release a burden they have been carrying. We visualized putting all of Gunny's liver disease

159

into the rock, and left his illness behind at the foot of the cross. For all I know, that is why he lived longer than any of Mark's other liver patients did. It is as good an explanation as any.

The great thing about pilgrims is that regardless of age, where you come from, or what you do for a living, most of us are just trying to find our way and stay on course—both metaphorically and literally. And to literally stay on the Path, you look for the symbol of the scallop shell or for the yellow arrows that are sometimes spray-painted on rocks and trees to point you in the right direction. You don't need a map; you just need to find and follow the yellow arrows. If you do that, you'll find your way.

In 2011, I hadn't walked the Camino for several years because of the boys' health issues—I just didn't feel that I could be away from them that long. Plus, I had been reluctant to leave Gunny's Rainbow in someone else's hands. Evidently, the Universe noted my prolonged absence from the Path, because the Camino came looking for me in Sanibel Island, Florida, to offer up some learning opportunities. I knew that because I was surrounded by its symbol: the scallop shell.

We ended up there at Gunny's suggestion. What he loved most was to be outside and take in all the sounds of nature. To do that in the winter, we were going to have to head south. And since Spain was not in the cards, we decided to go to Sanibel's dog friendly beach to enjoy one another's company for a few weeks, although *we* was not going to include Juan Carlos for most of that time because of his coaching schedule.

One of the things motivating us to take this vacation was that Gunny had developed a new tumor in his liver that we were not going to do anything about. When he decided to have the splenectomy, he made it very clear that it would be his last medical procedure. "*I don't care what goes wrong next. We're not fixing it.*" I not only respected his decision, it came as a relief from the life or death decision-making that had been our constant companion for so many years. While it was logical to assume that Gunny did not have a great deal of time left, I was the last person to ever predict or underestimate him. Nonetheless, better to go on vacation sooner rather than later, so off we went to Sanibel Island in January 2012.

My contribution to Gunny's vacation plan was to stop in Gainesville, Florida, which is directly on the route, to repeat a CT scan for Bacchus and see Dr. Nick for an evaluation. I was expecting to get a stamp of approval and be on our way because Bacchus looked and felt great. I was therefore stupefied when the CT scan showed three tumors in Bacchus' right lung, all of which had appeared since October 31st when he had last posed for the CT camera. The tumors were "weird" to the doctors. Why were all three in one lung lobe, giving us the possibility of surgery to cut them out? What if they were unrelated to his prostate cancer and not metastases, but rather a new and different cancer, which was likely more treatable? The questions and possibilities seemed endless. *What on earth were we supposed to do now?* Not even his doctors could agree on that.

My short-term answer was, "Continue on to Sanibel." We had come to Florida for a much-needed vacation. Three tumors in Baco's lung didn't change that. In fact, they were probably the best argument in favor of taking a time-out to enjoy ourselves as a family and just play.

Bacchus adored running on the beach, swimming, and rolling in the sand until his black fur turned white like a polar bear. He swam twice a day in Sanibel, retrieving his ball from the Gulf and bounding through the sand, laughing nonstop. While he exercised, Gun lay in the sand, watching Bacchus do his thing, listening to the waves and staring in wonder at the giant brown pelicans, which even his old eyes could see. He also enjoyed all the people on the beach stopping to chat with him. He generated a lot of attention because he arrived at the beach every day in his little red wagon, pulled by yours truly, and was outfitted in his fashionable red harness so I could hold him when he walked on the beach . . . wearing his little purple rubber booties that protected his tender old feet from all those scallop shells. We were quite a sight! While I didn't particularly enjoy people asking how old he was and then offering up how their dog had died at that age, we both enjoyed all the love and attention he got from total strangers.

One afternoon when I was helping him to walk back to the red wagon, a woman sitting on the beach called out, "Oh my goodness, he is so beautiful." I almost burst into tears. It was always lovely when someone saw his beautiful spirit, not just an old dog struggling to make his way through the sand.

I still had to decide what to do about Bacchus. At times I thought I should not do anything in terms of medical intervention and just let Bacchus enjoy what was left of his life. I had done my best for him and maybe it just didn't work out as we had hoped. Were his tumors meant to be a teaching

162

moment for *me*? Was this my opportunity to learn to let go and not fight so hard like I had done for years with Gunny? Maybe it was just horrible cancer, nothing more, nothing less, and there was no lesson to learn at all. I honestly didn't know. At my request, Alexandra talked to Bacchus' spirit guides to ask them if surgery was in Bacchus' best interest (however one wishes to define that). The answer was, "No."

I cried every day in Sanibel at the thought of Bacchus' life being cut short. I had always thought I would have time with him after Gunny died, when we could spend more time one on one and I could really know him better. He was an interesting little guy, my baby boy, and he had lived in the shadow of all of Gunny's challenges for most of his life. I was looking forward to helping him off the floor one day as an old man and stroking his gray beard, just as I was doing with Gunny. And now, unimaginably, I faced the possibility of Gunny outliving him.

I don't remember now if I "decided to decide" what to do about Bacchus before or after Gunny had a stroke in Sanibel. It is all a bit of a blur. I had brought Gun in from a short evening walk, and the next thing I knew, he was unconscious. His third eyelid was up, eyeballs somewhere else, and he was just gone.

I knew immediately that it was another stroke. There was nothing to do, nowhere to go. No reason to believe that he would benefit from medical attention. So, I waited. I periodically yelled his name and shook him, and sometimes he seemed to come back for a second, then he was gone again.

Mark just happened to call in the middle of all this, wondering how we were doing. My answer was to the point. "I am sitting here waiting to see if Gunny wakes up from the stroke he just had." He was shocked, but confirmed the wisdom of doing nothing.

About an hour later, Gun lifted up his head, yawned, and put it back down. Then a few minutes later, he woke up like nothing had happened, drank some water, and within thirty minutes was woofing at me to feed him dinner. Seriously. Alexandra called about the same time because he had popped in to say, "*Hi,*" and she was wondering what was happening in Florida. When she asked him how he had recovered so quickly, he told her, "*I didn't want to miss my vacation.*" The yellow arrow was nowhere in sight.

I asked the Universe to please let me know what was best for Bacchus when I woke up the next morning. When I woke up at 3:30 a.m. to turn and feed Gunny, I was crying in my sleep, in the middle of a dream. In my dream, Bacchus was dead. I didn't even know how he died, but I knew he was dead and Gunny was still alive.

I lay back down in bed, thinking that was my answer. He was going to die before Gunny. Evidently, I needed to let go and accept what was happening and just love and support him as best I could. I didn't know how he had died in the dream; I just knew he was gone.

I went back to sleep, and when I woke up in the morning, I was crying again—half asleep, half awake. The dream had totally changed course. In my dream, it was now two days after Bacchus had died and I went to the hospital and said, "I need to see him. I didn't tell him goodbye and I want to hold him."

When I arrived at my "dream" hospital, I went to the table where he was lying and held him . . . and he started licking my face. I ran over to get the doctor and I said, "Oh my God. He's not dead! Come quick. You have to help him!"

They told me I was wrong and that I "needed to accept" that he was dead. (Why do people always say this to me both in my dreams and in my real life?) By this point he was actually clawing at me and acting almost feral. They saw that he was alive, and said nothing except, "It's not possible." And then I woke up completely.

It was my dream so I got to interpret it. I decided that my dream was telling me that there was a chance. Maybe there was a path that led to Bacchus waking up and licking my face because he had survived even when everyone thought he was dead. I was not supposed to just accept his diagnosis any more than I had ever accepted one of Gunny's. I felt I had found the yellow arrow pointing the way.

We went back to Gainesville for Nick to remove part of Bacchus' lung. I did it despite what Alexandra had told me Bacchus' guides had said, and despite the fact that I knew medical treatments were very upsetting to him. I did it against Gunny's wishes as well. One of Gunny's and my last fights was over Bacchus' lung surgery. He had told Alexandra that Bacchus would not want the surgery, that all they wanted was to be together, and that Bacchus would *want to go out on a high note.* It made me furious. As I explained to him, nobody goes out on a high note unless they get flattened by a car while playing Frisbee—and the chance of that happening to one of my dogs was nil.

I thought, "How could he be so cavalier about Bacchus' life when he had fought so hard for his own over and over again?"

Turns out, there was only one tumor in Bacchus' lung, not three as the CT picture had suggested, and it had nothing to do with his prostate cancer. It was a new and different cancer—and in keeping with the ridiculous nature of all my dogs' illnesses, a type of cancer not reported in a dog's lung since the 1960s—and was likely cured by simply removing it. Bacchus was going to be okay. When Nick called to tell me Bacchus was being released from the hospital, and I told Gunny, he got his tired old body off the floor unassisted, grabbed my shoe, and danced around the room with the shoe in his mouth. They just wanted to be together. Always.

I now know that if we had not removed part of Bacchus' lung, that cancer probably would have killed him around the time that Gunny died. The fates had not intervened with Bacchus' path, I had. Did I make the right decision? That depends. Right for whom? Me? Bacchus? Gunny? Juan Carlos?

When I was in Sanibel, I thought the arrow was pointing me to surgery. Two years after the fact, I am not so sure. Perhaps I should have just let them die together. Maybe their words, not my dream, were the yellow arrow pointing the way. Bacchus loved Gunny more than anything, so who was I to say he should have to experience the agonizing loss of his best friend? Why did I think that I knew better than everyone, including Bacchus, what was best? Why was I so willing to give Gunny the power to make decisions about his medical care, but didn't extend the same courtesy to Bacchus?

In part, I did not defer to Bacchus because he did not have the life experience and maturity of thought that Gunny did. He was more like a young, innocent child in many ways. But maybe even a young child knows what is best for his own soul, as opposed to his life expectancy. Our job as Bacchus' guardians was to do what was best for *him*, and I fear we chose what was best for *us* instead — even if we were not conscious of it at the time. As sure as I am of every decision I made for Gunny, I worry that putting Bacchus through that surgery — and all the things that came later — was truly my biggest mistake. And yet I also know that Bacchus forgives us for doing it because he knows that we did it out of love for him.

We returned home from Florida in February 2012. Bacchus was such a sweet and loving boy that he did what his mom and dad asked him to do. He recovered from his surgery. He lived. And he continued to bring joy to our house.

Unfortunately, Gunny did not really have many good days after we returned. He was tired and sick, and spent a lot of time sleeping and dreaming and just generally being out of his body whenever he could. But he did have a great last vacation in Sanibel, even considering the stroke.

Chapter 24

I never thought I'd have such an interesting life as a dog. I realized lately that Laurie has given me the opportunity to experience life from a different perspective, that of a chocolate brown Lab to be precise. For the most part [I am not happy to be a dog] because as I stated before, I don't have control over my life. But I can't say it's been all bad. For one thing, I probably wouldn't have lived my life with Laurie, gotten to know her, learned all I have this time around. And who knows what kind of life I would have had [if I hadn't been a dog] – or more likely would not have been here at all.

How I have changed. It would probably never have happened if I had been a man again so soon. Only in this dog skin, with its limitations, could I have ever come to realize so much. I want to leave my mark and know there was a reason for my life. I want to do better next time around if there is a next time. Will I come back to earth and be a man again? I wonder. It's unnerving sometimes because I really don't know what is in store for me after I leave my home here. I think about that a lot. This divine plan might know what it's doing after all. Just maybe.

169

I don't long to go but know it will happen soon enough. I'm tired of my fragile physical state. It has become very difficult. I worry about Laurie, Juan Carlos, and Bacchus. I wonder if they will follow their dreams and make the most of their lives.

Ganimedes

As Gunny has mentioned several times now, over time, he began to remember his past lives as a man. I think it all started when he saw himself in that puddle when he was two years old, saw the reflection of a dog, and thought, *"That can't be me. I'm a man."* I'm sure it took years to process that, and at the time it happened, he had no one to talk to. He was alone with his thoughts, struggling with what he called *"the duality of my nature."* By this, he meant the fact that he understood he was in a dog's body, with animal instincts and emotions, and an intense connection to other animals. Yet he was simultaneously conscious of the fact that he had a soul, a purpose in this life, and the thoughts and experiences of a man. And as he entered the twilight of his life, he reflected more on how being an animal differs from being a human being, his present life as a dog, his past lives, and what might be awaiting him on the other side:

You asked, 'What is life's purpose as I see it?' Interesting question. One thought up by someone other than a dog.

Some dogs are given tasks to do, some are trained for their owners to command, some dogs are given the job of companionship, some are mistreated and neglected, some take off on their own or try to. I would imagine the answer would be very subjective but I want to think about why dogs are so loyal to their companions, especially when mistreated. Does it go beyond necessity? I know in my case (I'm not mistreated) it is partly because of instinct and partly because of an internal mutual attraction and need to love and be loved. So one conclusion is there is something in our core that instinctually makes us trust and love until proven otherwise but even still we persist as any abused being, human or animal, even when it may become unbearable. Have we become so inbred that we've lost our instinct for freedom? Are we too scared to fend for ourselves? Would we ever have the freedom to do that?

I feel indebted to the animal community I share here in Bethesda, Maryland, and on earth too. I would have liked to go to Africa and meet elephants and kangaroos — well, almost any wild animal where they live in nature. I saw many on TV and find them interesting. I have become more curious about animals and look at them differently now that I am one.

I am just beginning to understand myself and there is so much more to learn. Humans are complicated.

Most animals are not. Maybe it's because animals don't pretend to be something they're not. They don't have hidden agendas and their basic desires are known. They are honest. They have no reason to lie. A predator is a predator. Humans may say one thing and mean another. We all have to find a way to survive, but animals have a clearer connection to the earth than most people have. They are aware of its heart, its pulse. They know when they are in sync or out of balance with nature. Of course most dogs are not in the kill-or-be-killed category but they are still able to communicate with their hearts and their minds. What's interesting to me is humans are evolving or not because of will and choice. Animals are evolving also. They have lost something too.

Gunny's answer to the question, "What is life's purpose as you see it?" surprised me because it focused entirely on the life of animals. It didn't focus on the purpose of his particular life, as an animal or otherwise, so much as the experience of being an animal in general. It makes sense to me that while a person might say that their "purpose" is to have a family, or a good career, or even to help other people or animals, perhaps a non-human animal's purpose is simply to live honestly, in harmony with nature and the world around them. I think people often confuse "purpose" with "goals", and Gunny's response reminds me that they are not the same thing. Perhaps animals like dogs, who spend a lot of time with people, are losing part of their true nature as they evolve with us. Perhaps we humans have already lost touch with our true nature more than any other species, by choice.

Gunny had not lived harmoniously with nature, or other people, in his past lives as a man. When he recalled those lives, it was never with pride, but more often with regret for the mistakes he made, as well as sadness about the actions of other people towards him.

I know life is never perfect. Will this knowledge allow me to forgive my trespasses in past lifetimes and my shortcomings in this one? When I was a sailor, I was very religious but not spiritual. I had religion beat into me as a boy, which is hard to believe since my father was a beast, a drunk, and cared for no one, least of all his children or his wife. My mother was nasty herself, and I think she enjoyed taking out her frustration on me also, until I grew too strong. I had many siblings, but my younger sister was frail and sweet, and I knew she wouldn't last long. When she died of brutality and ill health, I finally found the courage to leave. I always felt a twinge of guilt for leaving my younger brother there. I knew it would be hard for him. I hoped my older sister would look out for him. I never saw any of them again.

I was maybe twelve or thirteen. I had saved a few shillings and hid some bread away and left one night. I remember cobblestone streets, the sound of horses' hooves, and dampness everywhere. I hid under a small rowboat on a ship and was beaten when found, but fortunately we were already at sea.

I worked hard, and as I became stronger and taller, I was given more opportunities to learn my eventual craft — that of making and repairing sails and line. I grew stronger and stronger, but after many years I was left in a port where I later found another ship. This time the captain wasn't so lenient. I left the first chance I got, jumping ship. I wasn't the only one, two of us stuck together until we found another ship. This time the captain and his men welcomed us aboard, asking what we had to offer. We were both strong. I had my craft, and he had a few tricks up his sleeve. He was crafty but always fair with me. He carved wood and bone.

We found out soon enough these men fought for whomever was willing to pay. As dangerous as my life had become, I flourished. I loved this life and couldn't imagine any other. Then eventually came a battle with another ship and the storm that took my life and that of many others. All I remember is the ship finally breaking apart, and I was thrown into a stormy sea. I know I was bleeding, but it was impossible to see anything. I grabbed hold of some wooden debris and made it to shore, but it was too late. I had lost too much blood and died. Again I was not a spiritual man, but I loved my life. I was not more than thirty when I died.

If I am to be a man again, I sometimes think I'd want a family, even though the great responsibility I feel when I think about it tugs at my heart and mind and makes me run away. Gunny never told Alexandra about a lifetime where he had a good family, love, and a peaceful life. Perhaps he had had such lifetimes, but never remembered them. Perhaps during the times that he lived, such a comfortable existence was rare. The only clue he gave us as to the time of any of those lives was the reference to shillings, which puts him in Great Britain between the early 1700s and the early 1900s. I do not imagine that many people were living fairy tale lives then.

Gunny's stories rang true for me, and for him, because many of his lifetimes seemed connected to his life as Ganimedes—regardless of the obstacles put in his path, he figured out how to get himself out of bad situations repeatedly and fought for his life until he died. And his love of the sea transcended lifetimes, from the life of a sailor to this life as a dog, where nothing pleased him more than a walk on the beach and feeling the sea spray in his face.

I love the beach even though sometimes it hurts my feet. The beach often smells like fish and other things to eat. It reminded me of [my] past life when I was on a ship at sea. I fought then, too. Have I always been a madman when I have been a man, fighting and clawing my way through life? I see the wind in the sails of the large vessel and it makes me excited to feel the wind hitting my face. (Make feeling the wind on my face the top of the list of my favorite things.) I loved the unknown, the adventure, moving from place to place. I see myself hanging on the rigging with the salty water on my face and tongue, my clothes clinging to my skin. I was always ready for a fight, for a new danger, excited for the rewards that waited for me on land.

Always a warrior of one kind or another. They were not lives that provided time for thought and reflection, and at various points he recognized that despite the downsides, his dog life *did* provide that opportunity. This life also provided him the opportunity to be loved and cared for in a way he never described in his past human lives. And he loved and cared for us with a depth he never describes feeling in other lives. He may have run away from those he loved in his past lives, but he was steadfast with his family in this one. And he was *never* an aggressor in his dog life. He was gentle with every being that he met, but had a will of steel.

What does it all mean? These other life times? This life time? I don't know. And as Gunny himself said to me not long ago, *"My life is not for you to figure out. It is for me to figure out. Your life is for you to figure out."*

176

Chapter 25

My life began a very long time ago as a man. I remember being a soldier of fortune, because the battalion of men I led looted many a city. I was a Roman general and remember with pride at that time to have been in such a high station because I wasn't born into a good family. I was very handsome and strong and the ladies flocked to me. I remember the armor I wore which was heavy on my chest and I know I did many things that I am no longer proud of, thus the reason I came back as Ganimedes the DOG. I know I have had many lives as a human being but [that] one is what brought me here.

There was a young girl once. She was walking just outside of town in the north. She was fair-haired and had pink cheeks. My men would have gladly had their way with her. I picked her up as I rode past her and carried her screaming into the town where I set her down and watched as she ran into the arms of her mother. My men and I kept going. It was one of the only nice things I did. I wasn't sure why then, but I know now it was Laurie and that is our connection from the past to the present.

*I hope Laurie realizes how amazing she is [in this life].
I think all these tests I put her through are part of our
preordained destiny together. We made a pact. I see
us wander through misty clouds with a thread-like
string attached from one to the other so we wouldn't
lose our way to each other in the mist of the afterlife
pit stop. After wandering for some time, I see us
finding each other. We had been children together in
another life. We were split apart by violence. We were
taken from our home that was burned to the ground
and I see some men putting me in a horse-drawn cart
and taking me away, my life given to the man our
father hurt. I see you [Laurie] staying in the village
with our mother. I believe our father had brought this
wrath down on us by taking this other man's son
from him, and this time our father ran away. You
eventually married and had many children and died
in childbirth. We had another brother who came to a
violent end early on when we were still a family. It
was an accident but I think that's what brought on
the feud.*

*I told you then that we would see each other again
and I meant it. That's when we made the pact. When
we met again in our Roman life we weren't given
the opportunity to be together except for that brief
encounter, but I suppose that was part of the plan.*

Ganimedes

I do not remember these lifetimes shared with Gunny. But I have always known that the connection we have is more powerful than anything I have ever experienced. I do believe that we made a soul pact at some time and place in the long distant past—I feel the "thread-like string" keeping us connected. I have always known, somewhere in my being, that he saved my life and that this time around, it was my turn to save his. When he speaks about our brief encounter in a Roman life, it resonates for me. He was the Roman soldier who saved my life as a young girl. Yet, he looks at it as the moment that I saved *his* soul because it was one of the only good things he ever did in that life.

In his last months, I gave myself over completely to loving Gunny, caring for him, and helping him struggle through every day. But at the very end of his life, it was extreme. I pretty much never left him, not even to go to dinner or a movie with friends. And I did not really maintain my relationship with anyone. The rest of the world just sort of faded into the background and all I did, all night and day, every day, was love and care for Gunny. It was not a sacrifice. There was nothing else that I wanted to do. In many ways, Gunny and I saved each other in this life, too, not just the Roman life. We opened our hearts and experienced together the beauty of unconditional love. And I had no idea how I was going to go on without him.

Chapter 26

Laurie is the wind that pushes the sail, the moon that pulls the tide and lights up the sky. She is my all and everything on this earth in this crazy life. I feel such an overwhelming debt of gratitude to her for saving my soul in that distant past and for enlightening my spirit every day in every way in this life. I have paid attention to her resolve, her integrity, her pain, her vision, and her gigantic heart. She breathes with me now as she has done for so very long. I don't even know if I could breathe on my own anymore. Her breath has become my breath, her wisdom my wisdom, her insight my heart.

Laurie has made me who I am today and has shared the depth of her soul with me, so now it is my turn. I love you Laurie and thank you forever for being so kind to me, so thoughtful, so giving of yourself. I know we have walked this walk together so many times. Why is letting go so difficult? Not just for you but for me also. I have to be honest about that. It hasn't only been your need for me to stay but mine also because I keep finding a new surprise around every corner in this amazing life I share with you.

We both have a choice, a say in our future together or apart. But I believe as before we are still held together by mutual love and will find each other again in the mist of eternity.

Remember when you promised me your heart if I would just stay a little longer? You said you would make it worth my while. Well, you came through every time. No dog could have a better friend and ally and no man could have a truer love. You watched and waited for me to grow and flourish as a more complete being, maybe not consciously, but what I have become and been able to accomplish even within the confines of this old body has been truly enlightening. A gift from God and you.

Funny I should say God. Although I don't really know what that is I believe there is one. There has to be a beginning somewhere in order for there to be an end. Thank you for saying I can go because I'm truly exhausted from holding on to this body. I leave it quite often now but when I wake I am still in it, or should I say back in it. I have asked the angels I see around me to let me know when it is time to go.

Maybe that's why we have more than one lifetime because it is impossible to accomplish everything put before us in just one. Maybe I started too late or compromised too many times, but I have done quite a lot in spite of my ignorance. It started as a lark, a lot of fun to be able to talk to people, get into their heads, and get the dogs thinking. But as time has gone on, I became more serious about my motives and direction. Having all this time to think things through and then act on them, bringing people together and helping others, has been fantastic. I've enjoyed doing something good. I know that is something that I have gratefully worked out. I know how lucky I have been to have shared my life with you and am glad to have been able to include others on this journey with us.

You are a great woman. I hope you will continue in confidence with anything you decide to pursue, but most of all, I hope that you find that peaceful place you sorely deserve.

Be happy, Laurie. You are worth it. Be kind to yourself.

I love you forever.

Ganimedes

Gunny's liver tumor had continued to grow and cause problems for him. He loved to eat more than almost anything, but it reached a point in the last week of his life where he was unable to enjoy a meal. Mark concluded that it was likely that the liver tumor, which was quite large now, was pressing on the nerve that controlled his ability to swallow. Poor Gunny would hungrily eat his food, and then be completely panicked because he was unable to properly swallow due to spasms in his esophagus. His got a petrified look in his eyes, drool coming out of his mouth, because the spasms would not allow him to swallow. It did not appear that he would really be able to eat anymore, much less enjoy it.

We tried different foods to see if he could swallow something better. Carol also taught me a technique to "reset" his swallowing reflex, which sometimes worked. But the reality is that there were not really any good moments in his day and he was getting progressively worse. He was so weak that we had to carry him outside to the bathroom and he needed help with every single aspect of his day to day life. It was painful to witness, and it was now clear that this time, he would not and could not rally.

He asked to be released from the body of Ganimedes the Dog on Easter Sunday, April 8, 2012. He was fourteen years, nine months, and five days old.

While I had planned to call Mark at some point the next day to tell him it was time, we were not able to wait. On Sunday, Gunny evidently had aspirated food into his lungs, which I did not realize until the middle of the night. I woke Alexandra up to ask her to please look at his energy and confirm that he had pneumonia. I really did not want to take him to the emergency room in the middle of the night, but if he had pneumonia, I could not risk having him feel like he was suffocating again, knowing how terrified he had been the last time. She confirmed that she saw ill energy in one of his lungs, and we knew that we could not wait.

I called Mark from the car at 5 a.m. on our way to Annapolis to tell him Gunny was ready. He needed Mark's help one last time. It was incredibly important to Gunny that Mark be the person to release him. He trusted Mark with his life, and he was the only person whom he trusted with his death.

We met Mark at the hospital, and I was desperately trying to figure out how to avoid this moment, how to postpone actually letting him go. "Maybe we could take him back home for the day, just for a few hours, maybe I would be more ready if I had a little more time."

Mark was pretty blunt. "You are not going to be any more ready in a few hours than you are now. You are never going to be ready. It is unlikely that he will live for more than thirty-six more hours, even if you try to treat the pneumonia — and they will not be good hours." There was no decision to make. It was just a matter of having the courage to do what was right. And what Gunny had asked us to do.

You may remember that I had told Gunny a long time before, when he was afraid of the ghosts, that they could not take him. That only God could take him from me, and that we would talk about it and we would know when it was time. I had also told him at various points that he was lucky he was a dog; people were required to suffer until they finally died, but dogs were allowed to die without suffering until the bitter end. He knew what euthanasia was and understood it.

Gunny was very clear that he did not want Bacchus to watch him die; it would be too traumatic for Bacchus. And although he would have liked for Juan Carlos to be with him, Juan Carlos just couldn't do it. So, he and Bacchus waited out in the car while Mark and I stayed with Gunny. There is nowhere else I wanted to be or could have been.

Gun understood perfectly what was happening, and he was quite calm and alert. When the moment came to give him the injection, he simply rolled onto his side on the blankets we had put down for him and closed his eyes. I lay on the floor with my arms around him, spooning him, and whispered, "You are the best thing that ever happened to me. When you leave my arms, you will be in the arms of your guardian angel, your pink lady, who will show you the way." And as he died, I told him, "I love you, I love you, I love you," a thousand times, nonstop, until I knew he could not hear me anymore. I asked Max and Diva and Winston, and my friend Susan who had died the year before, to please be there to meet him. As silly as it sounds, I was worried about how he would get along without me — I had been caring for him for so long I didn't really trust anyone else to do it. Not even God, I suppose.

I wish that I could tell you that there was something magnificent or beautiful in his death. A sign. Something memorable. There wasn't. It just was. What I felt more than anything was his relief that he could leave that broken body and stop fighting. He did not leave his body immediately, though. Long after he stopped breathing, he felt just as palpably present to me as he had when he was alive — as much as he wanted the physical release, he had been fighting to stay in his body so long I don't know if he was sure *how* to surrender. Mark and I stayed together for a good five minutes, talking about how extraordinary he was, and he was still present with us in the room, along with his body.

I wasn't actually in the room when his spirit left. I went to tell Juan Carlos and Bacchus that it was over, and when I returned to the room a few minutes later, Mark looked at me, tears in his eyes, and said, "He just left."

As Gun told Alexandra after he died, leaving us was the hardest thing he had ever had to do. It broke his heart to leave his family. Maybe he waited until I was out of the room because it was just easier to go without me there, emotionally still holding on to his body even though it was no longer alive.

Faith said she saw a rainbow that morning, which she always associates with him. Carol said she knew he was dead before I called her because he came to show her how easily he could move around now that he was out of his body. Shortly after he died, Gunny told Alexandra that he was in a beautiful place where the sky was multi-colored and sang to him. From the moment he died, he no longer appeared to her as a dog, but rather as a tall man wearing a long coat. Bacchus told her that Gunny appeared to him as a man, as well.

I was envious of all of them. I didn't see anything except a deep, dark, bottomless well of grief.

Chapter 27

What do you miss most about being alive?

Laurie

I *am* alive.

Ganimedes
November 22, 2012

It has been a year and a half since Gunny left his chocolate Lab costume. Many days are unbearably difficult. I think about him every day; I cry many of those days. Juan Carlos and I have been to the Camino twice since he died, looking for an arrow to point the way out of our grief, trying to go on. I walked for two hundred miles and followed all the yellow arrows, but the tears never stopped and I did not find my way.

We left most of his ashes in a few beautiful spots along the Path. It was Gunny's idea for me to put his ashes in a wheat field since he thought having part of him become a baguette — his most favorite food — was irresistibly funny. I also left some of his ashes in a beautiful river under an old Roman bridge in Estella, one of our favorite towns on the Path. The bridge seemed to be a nice tip of the hat to his Roman life, and leaving him in a river to swim was my way of poking fun at the fact that he made me build a pool and yet hated to swim.

We brought the remainder of his ashes to the beach in front of our house in Spain—his favorite place on earth—to spread them in the water lapping up on the shore.

Gunny was with me on the Camino; we walked side by side, *"breathing together as one."* Now it is he who breathes for me in some moments, not vice versa. We walked the Path together, just as we walked together most every day for fifteen years. Except now, he is a tall man who puts his arm gently around my shoulders to comfort me, and tells me not to worry, that he will wait for me. He doesn't appear as a dog, although he does still let me call him Gunny.

I have days when I read the things that Gunny wrote and I wonder, "How could it be real? He was a dog. I have pictures!" I am still a lawyer with a rational mind, and although my heart never questioned what Alexandra transcribed, my brain still struggled with the seemingly "unreal" nature of all that he said and the fact that he said it. Gunny knew I was struggling, and he gave me the proof I had been seeking a year and a half after he died.

I wasn't kidding when I said I was skeptical of most psychics. Alexandra is about the only one that I trust, and I've really never been to see anyone else. But a friend of mine insisted that I go see a medium who was in town, whom she swore was the real deal. I let her make an appointment, and I tried to bring my open mind with me. Justin, the medium, did not know my name. We had never met.

The conversation went something like this:

"Please say your name."

"Laurie Plessala Duperier."

"Please say, 'It's a beautiful day today.'"

"It's a beautiful day today."

"What is your month and day of birth?"

"07/15."

"Okay, the way I calculate numerology, your number is one because you have already had your birthday this year. For me, the number one signifies new beginnings, a fresh start, a new chapter."

"Okay. Sounds good."

"Wait a minute, this is very strange . . . I don't understand . . . it is very peculiar. I don't usually say that." Long pause, while staring a hole through me. "Are you writing a book?"

"Yes."

"Okay, then that is why I said, 'new chapter.' I never say that to people when I am describing what the numbers mean. I give the same description almost verbatim every time. But I must have said it because you are writing a book.

Now, I have your grandmother here. Your father's mother. She shows me a scene from *Mary Poppins* where Mary is measuring the children, and she says, 'Practically perfect in every way.' Your grandmother has a measuring tape across your book and that's what she says, 'Practically perfect in every way.'"

"That's nice."

"Did you call her Granny?"

"No, we called her Mom."

"Oh. [Pause. Speaking to someone other than me] You'll have to give that to me again. [Another pause] It's *Gunny*, not Granny. I have Gunny here. Who is Gunny?"

"He was my dog, and he is my soulmate."

"He is male?"

"Yes."

"You say he was your dog?"

"Yes."

Pause. "I am confused. It is very strange. I don't think this has ever happened. He does not come to me as a dog. He comes to me as a man."

"I know. That is why I'm writing the book. He was a man in his other lifetimes and got sent back as a dog this time. He wasn't very happy about it and doesn't plan on doing it again."

"I do have a dog here. He's running around and is very happy. I'm not sure of his name, but it starts with the letter B."

"That's Bacchus. He was my other dog."

"Well, it doesn't matter how Gunny appears, souls are souls, and we're all connected to the same consciousness."

"I know. That's what Gunny says. It is a quote from him in my book."

"What? Oh. Right. He tells me that he is giving you those words because he wants you to know that it was all real. It all really happened. Everything he said to your friend was real. You should not doubt that. He is with you all the time, you know. Do you feel him?"

"I feel him a lot of the time, especially when I am working on our book."

"He says to tell you that when you think you see him out of the corner of your eye, it is him. And when you think he is there, he is.

He says one more thing. He says, 'Tell her that she still has me.'"

"I know that I do."

And with that I left the table, crying. I felt tremendous relief to hear Gunny's voice, and joy to know that he and Bacchus were okay. But I also felt trepidation at the magnitude of what had just happened. The little escape hatch in my head that occasionally allowed me to pretend that this was all just a figment of my imagination when I felt overwhelmed by what the truth really meant, was now forever irrevocably closed. My mind had no choice but to join my heart in knowing that something extraordinary had happened in my otherwise very ordinary life. And I was in fact going to tell the world about it, regardless of what the world thought about it or me.

Chapter 28

I know now for certain, whether human or animal, we are made of the same stuff, the same consciousness. A soul is a soul and my advice to people everywhere is, 'Do your homework.' Find out who you are and who you want to be inside. To most humans I say, 'Wake up.' The clock is ticking. Be aware. Be awake. Care more about all of humanity. Care about your home, Mother Earth.

Don't be the same person you started as at the end of your journey in this life. Let yourself be fragile so you can open yourself up to all the beauty that's around you. Don't give up on yourself when things get tough. Don't give up on others. Don't have a closed heart or a closed mind. Be kind, be generous with what you have to offer others, be courageous, and be whoever you truly are.

Ganimedes

Epilogue

It is very simple. When your soulmate dies, you have a choice. You can choose to look forward to life, or you can choose to look forward to death.

Rose the Shaman
October 10, 2013

In the days, weeks, and months after Gunny died, I woke up every morning hoping that maybe today was the day that I would finally feel better. That the weight of my grief would start to lift. To console me, friends told me that it would take time, that time heals everything. It did not heal me. I never seemed to feel better.

The first night after Gunny died, I slept in his bed just so I could be surrounded by his smell. His scent was the only thing I could hang on to, the thing that made it seem like he was still physically here. In the following days, I learned that grief can literally bring you to your knees—my knees buckled one day, just walking down the hall, when a tidal wave of grief came over me. I ended up in the fetal position on the floor in the hallway, sobbing. And for weeks after he died, I would wake with a start at 4 a.m., thinking I had overslept his feeding time in the night. I started writing this book about six weeks after he died, hoping that it would help me heal, but I cried all over the keyboard for most of the day. While writing about the sad things was awful, I sometimes cried as much while writing about the happy things because those were the things that I missed most, like the flamenco singing, or barking at the boat, or the look of ecstasy on his face when he closed his eyes at the beach and felt the sea spray on his face. The memories just caused my soul to ache for him more.

When my despair is overwhelming, I still call out to him, and he comes as soon as he can, much like his "pink lady" used to come to him when he was scared. He must have read the letter I wrote to him five days before he died, where I said, "I wish that I could have the privilege of taking care of you for the rest of my life, but I know that is not how it goes. So I think that you will have the privilege of taking care of me from another place for the rest of my life. At least I sure hope so."

Juan Carlos was heartbroken at losing Gunny, but as I think is usually the case, people grieve differently and in their own time. In some ways our grief brought us together, and in other ways it separated us. After all, it must be strange for a husband to watch his wife grieve the loss of her soulmate. But truly, how many people marry their soulmates? The answer, I think, is not many. But that does not mean that it was easy for him to watch me love Gunny in a way that I could not love anyone else, or to watch the devastation it wrought when Gunny was gone.

The only thing worse than my own grief, was watching Bacchus grieve. He aged ten years overnight. The pup who was always ready to go for a walk and retrieve his ball didn't even want to get out of his bed. And my grief compounded his because he was so worried about me. He would sit in front of my desk for hours while I worked or wrote, and would not leave me. His happy face was now marked by a furrowed brow. He even walked like an old dog, not the jock he had been before Gun left.

Ultimately, his grief took a toll on his health. His prostate cancer, which had been firmly in remission a week after Gunny died, came back with a vengeance shortly thereafter. On August 22, 2012, Mark gave me the bad news that it had returned. On that day, I stopped grieving Gunny and put down my writing pen. I would not write another word of this book as long as Bacchus was alive. Instead, I turned all my energy to caring for Bacchus. He needed me, and this time, for once, I could be there for him fully and completely.

We went to Florida for more radiation treatment on his prostate, where they found that the cancer had spread to his bladder and he also had a potentially life-threatening tumor on one adrenal gland. I considered just turning around and going back to Washington, but I was conditioned to fight. So, Bacchus and I stayed in Florida for a couple of weeks and we irradiated all of his tumors, trying to buy him some more time.

There were lots of unforeseen complications, and while he definitely had some very good time in the months after we returned from Florida, he was never the same. He did, however, swim every single day, up until a week before he died. I had always known that when Bacchus no longer wanted to swim, he was finished with life, and that is exactly what happened. He died on March 14, 2013.

In the end, it was Bacchus, not Gunny, who made medical history and who contributed greatly to science. Because of the treatment he received and the sacrifices that he made, he lived for twenty-one months with a disease that, left untreated, normally kills a dog in just a few. He did it for only one reason: because we asked him to do it. He would have preferred to join Gunny in the Big Dream long before.

I understood his feelings completely. When I woke up on March 15th without either of my boys, I had double grief. All the grief about Gunny that I had suppressed to focus on helping Bacchus, along with the grief about losing Bacchus, flooded over me. I functioned — I swam dogs and went to the grocery store and smiled politely while having dinner with friends — and I also cried every day. I just never seemed to be able to feel joyful. I have to say, though, that all the things my friends had told me about time healing all wounds seemed to happen where Bacchus was concerned. I could feel that he was okay, that he was happy with Gunny in the Big Dream. Before too long, I was able to smile at a happy memory of him swimming in the pool or trotting down his favorite path, his ears bouncing up and down and a smile on his face.

But where Gunny was concerned, it was a different story. No matter how many miles I walked on the Camino and no matter how many tears I cried, the heartache just never seemed to ease. That year, I softly sang happy birthday to myself when I woke up, and then immediately thought, "Oh good. I am one year closer to being dead and being able to see Gunny again." I was not suicidal, I just longed for the day I would see him again. I also decided that August 22,

2013, one year after I had stopped writing to care for Bacchus, would mark the end of my writing hiatus. I started writing again several days a week as planned, and although I made progress on the book, I still didn't feel any better.

To make matters worse, in the months after Bacchus' death, I had a recurring leak at my pool that was becoming a threat to the continuing operation of Gunny's Rainbow. To repair it once and for all, we ultimately had to break out a foundation wall of the house. But once that leak was finally fixed, a new leak sprang in a different pipe every few days. I was at the end of my rope, questioning what on earth the Universe was trying to tell me by torturing me with a leaky pool. Alexandra suggested that I call Rose, the shaman, to see if she could help. So I did.

Rose and I spoke on the phone for about fifteen minutes, and I explained what was going on at my house. I told her I thought I must have another spirit problem, and I hoped that she could come fix it like she did the last one. She asked me a series of questions, and she then gently informed me that I did not have a spirit problem with my pool. Rather, it sounded to her like my leaky pool was a reflection of me, and until I fixed me, I was not going to fix my pool. As much as I hated to accept it, I knew that she was right. I was broken, and none of my efforts to fix myself had worked. Pretending not to be broken didn't make me *not* broken, as my pool constantly reminded me. It really wasn't so much pretending, though, as it was believing that I would just have to live for the rest of my life with the sadness about losing Gunny. I had accepted that was my fate. But Rose suggested maybe there was another possibility. Maybe I could release my grief and heal.

I made an appointment to see her for healing work, not knowing exactly what that would entail, and from the day that I made the appointment, my pool stopped leaking. (And it has not leaked again.) Gunny came with me to my appointment with Rose, and the first thing she said, not surprisingly, was, "You know he is a man, not a dog? He is very tall and very handsome." Yes, so I've been told. "He is desperate for you to be happy, and will do absolutely anything to help."

He and Rose took me to a place where I could start to release my grief, which generated the type of wailing and unnatural sounds that I associate with childbirth. Only when it was over, I did not have a bundle of joy to hold. It was just scary, painful, difficult, and sad. But it was a start. I felt a trickle of light start to flow into my heart, much the way Gunny saw a trickle of light come into his head when he was in the dark tunnel with pneumonia, and he felt everyone praying for him and willing him on. This time, Gunny was willing *me* on, and helping the trickle of light find its way into my heart, to bring it back to life.

Rose helped me understand that losing my soulmate was truly a pain like no other. It is not that I loved Gunny more than Bacchus or more than other people whom I had loved and lost, it was that when I lost him, I had lost the person who completed me, who made me feel whole. And who loved me unconditionally just as I was, good parts and bad.

Gunny's soul and mine must have needed to experience profound and abiding love. So we found each other again across the mist of time, and took the forms that allowed us to achieve that. Had we both been people or both been dogs, I do not think it would have happened. Gunny certainly seemed to doubt his ability to be a good "man" and to really love and care for a family as a man. I do not doubt his ability to do that all. I hope that in his next life, if he is a human, he will try and will succeed in loving as beautifully and completely as he did in this life.

I don't think there is a shrink alive who could have done for me what Rose did that day. She empowered me to make a choice to look forward to the rest of my life, and in the process helped me understand that without really knowing it, I had in fact been looking forward to death so that I could be with him again. That was a really awful thing to realize, but it was true.

Gunny has been with me while we wrote our book, helping along the way. But now it is done, and I know it is time to move on. I do not know what the next phase of my life will look like, and I find the idea of moving on to be mildly terrifying. But I have promised Gunny that I will choose to look forward to life. And I always keep my promises. On the days when it seems too hard, I will think of Bacchus, and I will do it anyway. Because Gunny asked me to.

CPSIA information can be obtained
at www.ICGtesting.com
Printed in the USA
FFOW02n1210011217
43877912-42872FF